LifeLight

"In Him was life, and that life was the light of men." John 1:4

Matthew Part 2

MATTHEW 13:53–28:20

LEADERS GUIDE

CPH
SAINT LOUIS

Jane L. Fryar, Editor

Revised from material prepared by Dale A. Meyer and Donna J. Streufert

This publication is available in braille and in large print for the visually impaired. Write to the Library for the Blind, 1333 S. Kirkwood Road, St. Louis, MO 63122-7295; or call 1-800-433-3954.

All Scripture quotations, unless otherwise indicated, are from the HOLY BIBLE, NEW INTERNATIONAL VERSION®. NIV®. Copyright © 1973, 1978, 1984 by the International Bible Society. Used by permission of Zondervan Publishing House. All rights reserved.

The verses so indicated are from the TODAY'S ENGLISH VERSION of the New Testament. Copyright © American Bible Society 1966, 1971, 1976. Used by permission.

The quotation marked KJV is from the King James or Authorized Version of the Bible.

Copyright © 2000 by Concordia Publishing House, 3558 S. Jefferson Ave., St. Louis, MO 63118-3968. Manufactured in the U.S.A.

All rights reserved. No part of this publication may be reproduced, stored in a retrieval system, or transmitted, in any form or by any means, electronic, mechanical, photocopying, recording, or otherwise, without the prior written permission of Concordia Publishing House.

Cover Illustration: Steve Edwards

Contents

Introducing the LifeLight Program			5
Session 1—Lecture Leader	Growing as Faithful Disciples	Matthew 13:53–15:39	9
Session 2—Lecture Leader	To Glory through the Cross	Matthew 16–17	15
Session 3—Lecture Leader	Helping Disciples Restore an Erring Brother	Matthew 18	20
Session 4—Lecture Leader	Preparing Disciples to Trust in God's Grace	Matthew 19–20	25
Session 5—Lecture Leader	The Disciples Learn to Talk about the Faith	Matthew 21–22	31
Session 6—Lecture Leader	Jesus Condemns His Unrepentant Opponents	Matthew 23	36
Session 7—Lecture Leader	Jesus Prepares Disciples for the End Times	Matthew 24–25	41
Session 8—Lecture Leader	Jesus Redeems Disciples in the Crisis of the Cross	Matthew 26–27	47
Session 9—Lecture Leader	The Resurrected Lord Sends Disciples with the Gospel	Matthew 28	53

Session 1—Small-Group Leader
    Growing as Faithful Disciples   Matthew 13:53–15:39   61

Session 2—Small-Group Leader
    To Glory through the Cross   Matthew 16–17   65

Session 3—Small-Group Leader
    Helping Disciples Restore an Erring Brother   Matthew 18   68

Session 4—Small-Group Leader
    Preparing Disciples to Trust in God's Grace   Matthew 19–20   71

Session 5—Small-Group Leader
    The Disciples Learn to Talk about the Faith   Matthew 21–22   75

Session 6—Small-Group Leader
    Jesus Condemns His Unrepentant Opponents   Matthew 23   79

Session 7—Small-Group Leader
    Jesus Prepares Disciples for the End Times   Matthew 24–25   82

Session 8—Small-Group Leader
    Jesus Redeems Disciples in the Crisis of the Cross   Matthew 26–27   86

Session 9—Small-Group Leader
    The Resurrected Lord Sends Disciples with the Gospel   Matthew 28   90

LifeLight Leaders Guide — Matthew Part 2

Introduction

Welcome to LifeLight

A special pleasure is in store for you. You will be instrumental in leading your brothers and sisters in Christ closer to Him who is our life and light (John 1:4). You will have the pleasure of seeing fellow Christians discover new insights and rediscover old ones as they open the Scriptures and dig deep into them, perhaps deeper than they have ever dug before. More than that, you will have the pleasure of sharing in this wonderful study.

LifeLight—An In-depth Study

LifeLight is a series of in-depth Bible studies. The goal of LifeLight is that through a regular program of in-depth personal and group study of Scripture, more and more Christian adults may grow in their personal faith in Jesus Christ, enjoy fellowship with the members of His body, and reach out in love to others in witness and service.

In-depth means that this Bible study includes the following four components: individual daily home study; discussion in a small group; a lecture presentation on the Scripture portion under study; and an enhancement of the week's material (through reading the enrichment magazine).

LifeLight Participants

LifeLight participants are adults who desire a deeper study of the Scriptures than is available in the typical Sunday morning adult Bible class. (Mid-to-older teens might also be LifeLight participants.) While LifeLight does not assume an existing knowledge of the Bible or special experience or skills in Bible study, it does assume a level of commitment that will bring participants to each of the nine weekly assemblies having read the assigned readings and attempted to answer the study questions. Daily reading and study will require from 15 to 30 minutes for the five days preceding the LifeLight assembly. The day following the assembly will be spent reviewing the previous week's study by going over the completed study leaflet and the enrichment magazine.

LifeLight Leadership

While the in-depth process used by LifeLight begins with individual study and cannot achieve its aims without this individual effort, it cannot be completed by individual study alone. Therefore, trained leaders are necessary. You fill one or perhaps more of the important roles described below.

The Director

This person oversees the LifeLight program in a local center (which may be a congregation or a center operated by several neighboring congregations). The director

- serves as the parish LifeLight overall coordinator and leader;
- coordinates the scheduling of the LifeLight program;
- orders materials;
- convenes LifeLight leadership team meetings;
- develops publicity materials;
- recruits participants;
- maintains records and budgeting;
- assigns, with the leadership team, participants to small discussion groups;
- makes arrangements for facilities;
- reports LifeLight activities and plans to the district's board of parish education, to the congregation(s), and to the district LifeLight director;
- communicates outreach opportunities to small-group leaders and to congregational boards;
- follows up on participants who leave the program.

The Assistant Director *(optional)*

This person may assist the director. Duties listed for the director may be assigned to the assistant director as mutually agreeable.

The Lecture Leader

This person prepares and delivers the lecture at the weekly assembly. **(Lesson material for the lecture leader begins on p. 9.)** The lecture leader

- prepares and presents the Bible study lecture to the large group;
- prepares worship activities (devotional thought, hymn, prayer), using resources in the study leaflet and leaders guide and possibly other, outside sources;
- helps the small-group discussion leaders to grow in understanding the content of the lessons;
- encourages prayer at weekly leadership team and discussion leaders meetings.

The Small-Group Coordinator *(optional; the director may fill this role)*

This person supervises and coordinates the work of the small-group discussion leaders. The small-group coordinator

- recruits with the leadership team the small-group discussion leaders;
- trains or arranges for training of the discussion leaders;
- assists the director and discussion leaders in follow-up and outreach;
- encourages the discussion leaders to contact absent group members;
- participates in the weekly leadership team and discussion leaders equipping meetings;
- provides ongoing training and support as needed.

The Small-Group Discussion Leaders

These people guide and facilitate discussion of LifeLight participants in the small groups. **(Lesson material for the small-group leaders begins on p. 59.)** There should be one discussion leader for every group of no more than 12 participants. The small-group discussion leaders are, perhaps, those individuals who are most important to the success of the program. They should, therefore, be chosen with special care and be equipped with skills needed to guide discussion and to foster a caring fellowship within the group. These discussion leaders

- prepare each week for the small-group discussion by using the study leaflet and small-group leaders guide section for that session **(see p. 61)**;
- read the enrichment magazine as a study supplement;
- guide and facilitate discussion in their small group;
- encourage and assist the discussion group in prayer;
- foster fellowship and mutual care within the discussion group;
- attend weekly discussion leaders training meetings.

Leadership Training

LifeLight leaders will meet weekly to review the previous week's work and plan the coming week. At this session, leaders can address concerns and prepare for the coming session. LifeLight is a 1½-hour program with no possibility for it to be taught in the one hour typically available on Sunday mornings. Some congregations, however, may want to use the Sunday morning Bible study hour for LifeLight preparation and leadership training. In such a meeting, the lecture leader and/or small-group coordinator may lead the discussion leaders through the coming week's lesson, reserving 5 or 10 minutes for problem solving or other group concerns.

While it requires intense effort, LifeLight has proven to bring great benefit to LifeLight participants. The effort put into this program, both by leaders and by participants, will be rewarding and profitable.

The LifeLight Weekly Schedule

Here is how LifeLight will work week-by-week:

1. Before session 1, each participant will receive the study leaflet for session 1 and the enrichment magazine for the course. The study leaflet contains worship resources (for use both in individual daily study and at the opening of the following week's assembly) and readings and study questions for five days. Challenge questions will

lead those participants who have the time and desire a greater challenge into even deeper levels of study.

2. After the five days of individual study at home, participants will gather for a weekly assembly of all LifeLight participants. The assembly will begin with a brief period of worship (5 minutes). Participants will then join their assigned small discussion groups (of 12 or fewer, who will remain the same throughout the course), where they will go over the week's study questions together (55 minutes). Assembling together once again, participants will listen to a lecture presentation on the readings they have studied in the previous week and discussed in their small groups (20 minutes). After the lecture presentation, the director or another leader will distribute the study leaflet for the following week. Closing announcements and other necessary business may take another five minutes before dismissal.

In some places some small groups will not join the weekly assembly because of scheduling or other reasons. Such groups may meet at another time and place (perhaps in the home of one of the small group's members). They will follow the same schedule, but they may use the music CD to join in singing the opening hymn and a cassette tape to listen to the week's lecture presentation. The tape and leaflets will be obtained from the director by the discussion leader. A cassette tape version of the lecture is available for purchase from CPH (see your catalog). Or a congregation may record the lecture given by the lecture leader at the weekly assembly and duplicate it for use by other groups meeting later in the week. Videotapes as well as audiotapes work well. If you can use a video camera to film the lecture, by all means do so.

3. On the day following the assembly, participants will review the preceding week's work by rereading the study leaflet they completed (and that they perhaps supplemented or corrected during the discussion in their small group) and by reading appropriate articles in the enrichment magazine.

Then the LifeLight weekly study process will begin all over again!

Recommended Study Resources for Matthew

Concordia Self-Study Bible, New International Version. St. Louis: CPH, 1986. Interpretive notes on each page form a running commentary on the text. The book includes cross-references, a 35,000-word concordance, full-color maps, charts, and time lines.

Franzmann, Martin H. *Follow Me: Discipleship According to Saint Matthew.* St. Louis: CPH, 1961. Reprint. Concordia Heritage Series, 1982. Now out of print, this classic by Professor Franzmann is a running exposition of Matthew's Gospel.

Lenski, R. C. H. *Interpretation of St. Matthew's Gospel.* Columbus, Ohio: The Wartburg Press, 1932, 1943. This older volume is a reliable, comprehensive, confessionally sound commentary by a Lutheran theologian.

Roehrs, Walter R., and Martin H. Franzmann. *Concordia Self-Study Commentary.* St. Louis: CPH, 1979. This one-volume commentary on the Bible contains 950 pages.

For the Director

The time has come to begin LifeLight—Matthew, Part 2. The effort you and other leaders have expended will now begin to bring results as students begin once more to address God's Word (and permit God's Word to address them) through individual study, in a small group, in the large-group presentation, and through review of the week's study.

As the second course gets underway, run through this final checklist.

- Were study leaflet 1 and the enrichment magazine sent or given to participants at least a week before the first assembly so participants could prepare for the small-group discussion?

- Is study leaflet 2 available for distribution at the close of the session?

- Are meeting places ready for each of the small groups? Are there enough chairs? Are the rooms clean, well-lighted, ventilated, and comfortably heated or cooled?

- Is equipment needed by the lecture leader ready?

- Are name tags ready for the participants? Remember that the names must be printed with large, clear letters.

- Are all participants assigned to small groups? How will participants find out of where their small groups will meet?

- Have you made preparations for the small groups that will be meeting separately from the large group assembly (perhaps in homes), including printed materials, name tags, a tape of the lecture presentation, and perhaps also music for worship?

Lecture Leaders Session 1 — Matthew Part 2

Growing as Faithful Disciples

Matthew 13:53–15:39

Preparing for the Session

Central Focus

This first session challenges the student to begin this course of in-depth Bible study with a desire for growth in faithful discipleship. The study should cause the student to look to Christ and to the biblical Word for growth.

Objectives

That the participant, as a child of God and with the Holy Spirit's help, will be led to

1. verbalize a personal need for an increase in faith;
2. demonstrate that only Christ and His Word provide a reliable guide for life;
3. cast a critical eye at contemporary religious notions and their influence;
4. be encouraged by biblical demonstrations of faith.

Note for small-group leaders: Lesson notes and other materials you will need begin on p. 61.

For the Lecture Leader

You are responsible for the worship that will begin each LifeLight assembly. Although you may share responsibility for worship at coming sessions with others, you will probably want to open the worship at this first assembly yourself. Have you arranged for a musician to play the opening hymn? Or will you use the music CD? If so, do you know how to operate the CD player and find the song quickly? Perhaps you might lead the assembly in reading the prayer in the study leaflet together. Whatever your plans, keep the opening to five minutes to allow the groups maximum discussion time. At this first assembly it may take participants a little longer to find the places where their discussion groups will meet.

Notice that the lecture presentation includes readings from Erskine Caldwell and Richard Baxter. Practice these readings with special care so you can present them effectively. Feel free to adapt the rest of the lecture to your own style. Add personal examples where you can, but watch your time. If you consistently begin and end LifeLight on schedule, participants will happily return.

Session Plan

Worship

Begin the session with a brief word of welcome. Express your joy and excitement in being able to study God's Word together with other believers. Then move into the hymn and prayer. The words of the hymn are printed in the study leaflet. Note that accompaniment for the hymn can be found on the music CD that accompanies this course. If you plan to use it, find the hymn on the disk and cue it up before class. After the hymn, read the prayer responsively, with the worship leader reading the first and third sections and the whole group the second and fourth sections.

Devotion

The four writers of the Gospels record nearly 40 parables our Lord Jesus told during His ministry here on earth. Matthew 13 includes seven of them. All deal with His kingdom. Let's zero in on that kingdom as we review the parable of the sower now. Listen to the words from verses 3–23. You may want to follow along in your own Bible. This process will help us connect LifeLight Matthew, Part 1, with Matthew, Part 2, as we begin to discuss it in this session. *(Read the text.)*

Imagine a garden plowed bare. Imagine cracks in the

earth an inch or so wide. Imagine soil so poor nothing will grow on it. What good would sunshine do in such a garden? No good at all. In fact, the sun will bake this garden further still. Sunshine will widen the cracks and harden the earth even more. Cloudy days can, in this sense, be seen as a mercy.

This picture illustrates one reason Jesus taught using parables. The unbelievers in his audience had already shut their hearts to the truth. More light would simply increase the hardness of their hearts and add to the punishment justice would demand. Jesus' method indicates the magnitude of His mercy. He taught in such a way as to shield them from receiving even more truth for which they would be held accountable.

Jesus' method also shows the magnitude of His mercy toward us! By His grace—and His grace alone—we have the ability to comprehend the truths He taught and to believe them. We are among those described in the first part of 13:12—we have already been given understanding and faith, and we can count on our Savior's promise to give us even more, to pour out understanding and faith in abundance! That will happen in this LifeLight course as the Holy Spirit works in our hearts through His Word. Where else do you see that happening in your life? Think about it!

Lecture Presentation

This lecture also appears on the CD-ROM that accompanies this course. Also look at the PDFFILES directory on the CD-ROM for overhead transparency graphics available for the course.

Introduction: Following Jesus Changes Us

Erskine Caldwell, recounting his days in Maine, recalls a conversation with a stubborn native.

"Well, Mr. Dolloff," I spoke up presently, "how much heating wood do you think I'll need for the winter?"

"The newcomers never do learn to know better," he said, as if I were the one who had changed the subject. "I'd favor making a God-given law against it."

"Against what?" I asked, curious about his remark.

"Painting a dwelling in the God-given State of Maine any color but white. It was Boston people who moved here and started doing it. First it was Swedes from Boston who bought a fine-painted white dwelling down the road from here and painted it as ugly yellow as anybody's old tomcat. Then it was that house where you live that was built to stay white and then was painted gray like a navy ship in Portland Harbor. Anybody but Boston people knows that white is the only God-given color for a respectable Down East dwelling to be."

Erskine Caldwell, " 'Down But Not Out' in Mt. Vernon, Maine," *Down East,* November 1987, p. 61.

Change is our topic. Not changes in society, like yellow or gray houses, e-mail, satellite TV, or what have you. The change we will talk about is far more personal: change in our attitudes and actions as we strive to catch up with Jesus Christ. Christ's call "Follow Me" means that we disciples are always striving to catch up with Him who leads us through life. Not that any of us will ever get ahead of the Master. He's the one who is always coaxing us to come farther down faith's road as we follow Him. He invites us to change, to react boldly and faithfully to whatever daily life throws our way.

How we do this, or don't do it, is what Matthew 13:53–15:39 is all about.

1 People Who Wouldn't Change

We'll start with negative examples, the people of Jesus' time who wouldn't change. As a first example, we'll look at hometown people, people as stubborn as Caldwell's Mr. Dolloff.

You'd expect the people of Nazareth to bubble over with enthusiasm for the local boy who made good. Jesus' miracles and authoritative teaching were well known. He was the kind of leader common people in common towns were waiting for. But no, not the natives of Nazareth (13:55). "Isn't this the carpenter's son?" they asked, perhaps recalling the old gossip about Jesus' parentage. No, they weren't going to let Him lead them into change. Put another way, they simply didn't believe.

Neither did King Herod Antipas. His reaction to John the Baptizer's prophetic call to change is a classic study in "turf protection." A siege mentality like Herod's is afraid to be challenged and is literally hell-bent on preserving the status quo. The turf that Herod wanted to protect was the false peace of mind that came from silencing dissent. It was easier for Herod to execute John, who had denounced his adulterous marriage to Herodias, than to confess his sin and start down the path of a changed life. So Herod dug his rut of lifelong habits even deeper. He executed John, and went on feeling content, satisfied with his life—until he began hearing fantastic reports about Jesus and His miracles. Then the old anxieties came to life again. Herod's conscience sprang to accuse him. Has John been raised from the dead? Herod wondered.

Display visual 1A from the CD-ROM here.

None of this should surprise us. Just being physically close to Jesus and the prophetic Word is no fail-safe guarantee of bold faith. If you and I don't receive Jesus' scriptural Word with repentant hearts and true faith, we continue the tradition of smug complacency and the security we feel in the status quo. No blessings. No change. In fact, our failure to grow in Christian faith and faithfulness will fuel the criticisms of those who believe that all Christianity does is to make people self-righteous and critical of others.

To be candid: Your participation in this Bible study is no automatic guarantee of growth in following Jesus. What will cause growth? Only the penitent prayer that God's Spirit draw you into more faithful discipleship as He touches your mind and heart through His Word!

2 Challenges to Change

The two feeding miracles, two of several stories in these chapters that use bread, teach us that following Jesus is sufficient for life. Both are stories of wherewithal. Remember Jesus' words from the Sermon on the Mount? "Take no thought, saying, What shall we eat? or, What shall we drink? or, Wherewithal shall we be clothed? ... Seek ye first the kingdom of God, and His righteousness; and all these things shall be added unto you" (6:31, 33 KJV). If we approach life as children of God happily following along behind the advancing strides of our Father, all other things, the molehills that sometimes look like insurmountable obstacles, will stop causing us so much anxiety. When the disciples saw no way to care for the crowds, Jesus seized the opportunity to teach them about His all-sufficient love.

Display visual 1B from the CD-ROM here.

Who among us would have suggested seating the crowd because we trusted the sufficiency of Christ? We all know the disciples' helplessness in our own terms. The family budget that becomes an ongoing story of too many bills, too little cash, and credit that is too seductive. Health is a precious blessing we appreciate most in its absence. Sometimes when it goes it does not return. Time is a physical problem. Either there is too little of it (often for young people raising families and pursuing careers) or there is too much of it (sometimes for the elderly who are unable to lead active lives any longer). Whatever the specific need you know firsthand, the story follows the same outline for us today as it did for the first disciples. Physical limitations pose stiff challenges—challenges to change, to leave behind the comfort of saying, "It can't be done." Can we instead boldly trust the competence and love of Christ?

There is more to these bread stories, however. Our discipleship does not involve following Jesus as some "bread king" (John 6:15), as a magician who indulges our important physical needs. No, we follow Christ because only He can change our hearts. The Pharisees and Sadducees, popular religious teachers of the day, appeared credible to people who sought spiritual guidance. Jesus, however, warned His followers about them, even as He traded sharp words with them. In a heated exchange (15:6), Jesus explained that the slavish obedience of the scribes and Pharisees to religious customs handed down from generation to generation really amounted to a sinful breaking of God's commands. Their religious traditions, like ceremonial hand washing (15:2), could not purify the heart. Only the teaching of God's Word can bring about that needed change. Obviously, Jesus' attack didn't set well with those religious leaders. The disciples, perplexed by the exchange, asked Jesus (15:12): "Do you know that the Pharisees were offended when they heard this?"

In next week's reading we will see how Jesus laid the truth out plainly for His followers, confused by His conflict with the religious teachers (16:11–12). " 'How is it you don't understand that I was not talking to you about bread? But be on your guard against the yeast of the Pharisees and Sadducees.' Then they understood that He was not telling them to guard against the yeast used in bread, but against the teaching of the Pharisees and Sadducees."

Just as yeast permeates dough, popular religious notions and human traditions can quietly infiltrate sound biblical doctrine. We Christians will readily oppose obvious evils like assisted suicide, abortion, drug abuse, and illicit sex. But more insidious is the yeast, those popular notions we adopt without checking them against God's Word.

"Why even consider doctrinal differences between churches? After all, we're all going to the same place, aren't we?"

"Let poor people pull themselves up like I did. Why should I care? Heaven helps those who help themselves, right?"

"I don't see any need to witness to my neighbors. They have their own ideas and they're moral people. Christians. Mormons. Jews. Followers of Islam. We all worship the same God in our own way."

The struggle between the insidious notions of our age, the yeast, and the clear words of Scripture clash just as sharply today as in Jesus' time. What Jesus plainly told His followers is still true. It is better to have God's gift of a clean heart and spiritual purity than a facade of contemporary religious wisdom that covers a heart unchanged by the Word. The bread stories, especially the teaching about yeast, give us a lot to think about.

3 Faith Is Demonstrated

Now come the bright spots of these chapters. Two demonstrations of faith will enable us to go home with positive encouragement as we stride after Christ.

First, be encouraged by the example of the Canaanite woman of 15:21–28. Jesus praised her (15:28): "Woman, you have great faith!" She was not a Jew. She was not an observer of the traditions of the fathers. She endured the rebuffs of the uncompassionate disciples. Still, she kept on insisting that Israel's Messiah could provide abundantly for Jew and Gentile alike.

Jesus Himself tested her. He used conventional religious prejudices when He said (v. 24), "I was sent only to the lost sheep of Israel." Then in verse 26 He put her off (notice as the bread theme comes up again): "It is not right to take the children's bread and toss it to their dogs." Jesus uses a word that refers to a family pet. It's a tender word and by it, He draws out from her own lips an expression of faith. Far from taking His words as an insult, she answers in a way that shows God's Word, not then-current religious beliefs, had produced God-pleasing faith in her (v.27): "Yes, Lord, … but even the dogs eat the crumbs that fall from their masters' table."

4 Consider Your Own Discipleship

Maybe you have felt that you are not in step with the "religious" people of your church. Maybe you felt hesitant about joining this in-depth Bible study. Maybe you said to yourself, "I wouldn't fit in. I don't know that much about the Bible." So here's your encouraging example as you start into this study. Though the Canaanite woman couldn't claim to have all the right prerequisites, she knew Christ could meet all her needs. That's true for you too. Friend, you can trust Him!

Some of you are more like Peter and the other disciples. You've heard all the conventional religious wisdom, you follow many human traditions, but you want to focus your life more clearly on Christ. Peter can encourage you. His walking on water is a testimony to what happens when disciples set their sights solely on following Christ. The sequel—Peter sinking—reminds us how easily faith can falter in the storms of daily life.

Peter was learning that following Christ meant stepping out in faith. For doing this, Peter deserves a pat on the back. Remember what Jesus said to the Canaanite woman? Good going, Peter! You stepped out of the boat in faith. Of course, it wasn't Peter who ultimately made those steps possible. Jesus, the object of Peter's faith, made it possible for Peter to walk on water. We know this because we know what happened soon after, in 14:30. Peter's own resources wouldn't hold him up. But Christ, the object of Peter's faith, brought divine deliverance.

What brought Peter down? "When he saw the wind, he was afraid" (14:30). The storm Peter saw produced fear. His senses evoked an emotional response. You know how that goes. The smell of a sizzling steak makes your mouth water. The sight of the couch after supper invites you to rest. A letter from the IRS produces … You understand! Our perceptions often trigger our emotions. God made both our senses *and* our emotions.

But sometimes this interaction leads us off the path. Faith, you see, does not depend on our emotions or on our perceptions, but on the external, eternal Word of God.

Display visual 1C from the CD-ROM.

Dr. C. F. W. Walther put it succinctly: "Feeling proceeds from faith, not faith from feeling" (*The Proper Distinction between Law and Gospel: Thirty-nine Evening Lectures* [St. Louis: Concordia, 1929] p. 201). Had Peter held on to the external word of Christ (v. 29), "Come," he would have reached Jesus on top of the water instead of sinking.

Peter's faith succumbed to sight. Where do your senses, your perceptions, lead you into doubt or unbelief? When do your emotions, rather than the promises of Christ, dictate your actions? By God's grace, we can let our Lord lead us to take bold steps of faith based on His Word, not on our perceptions or our emotions. Since our purpose in Bible study is that God's Spirit change us into ever more faithful followers of our Savior, let's take a moment to consider sight and faith in our own discipleship.

Someone slights you. How do you respond? Shoot straight from the hip (an emotional response), or address the offense based on scriptural meditation and Christian advice?

You're along in years, and it seems inevitable that you'll need to enter a nursing home. You're scared. What will control your attitude? Your fears? Or Jesus' promise in 28:20, "I am with you always"?

There is no need to multiply examples. We humans are a marvelously created combination of intellect and passion, of idealism and reality. Countless times in life we must respond to circumstances imposed upon us from the outside. Our response can be based on our feelings, feelings not sanctified by God's Word. The Pharisees did that. Their religious traditions were rationalizations of their own sinful natures. Our goal, however, as disciples hurrying after Christ, is to let the objective Word of God sanctify our perceptions and inform our emotions. Unless you have a halo on your head, you—and I—have plenty of room for personal growth as we strive to follow Christ. Like Peter, we walk by faith; if we attempt to walk by sight we will surely sink.

Conclusion

Richard Baxter was an English minister in the 17th century. His book, *The Saints' Everlasting Rest*, has been a devotional companion to many Christians. Baxter writes:

> *Do I set upon this work in my own strength, or rather in the strength of Christ my Lord? And "cannot I do all things through him that strengthens me?" Was he ever foiled by an enemy? He hath indeed been assaulted, but was he ever conquered? Why, then, doth my flesh urge me with the difficulties of the work? Is any thing too hard for Omnipotence? May not Peter boldly walk on the sea, if Christ gave the word of command? If he begin to sink, is it from the weakness of Christ, or from the smallness of his faith?*

Richard Baxter, *The Saints' Everlasting Rest* (London: The Epworth Press, 1962).

We set out on this study of Matthew looking ahead to the strength of Christ our Lord. May the Spirit of God use our studies to coax, cajole, push, prod, and change us more and more to a single-minded devotion to Jesus!

Concluding Activities

Distribute study leaflet 2 and encourage participants to read "Getting Started" on page 3 of the enrichment magazine.

Notes

Faced w/ insurmountable
sit down + be expectantly

Help us rely on the external word to build our faith than our emotions or perception

Help us discern the way we embrace relig tradits + cultural over your Word

As we start this second half of Matthew, show us where we need to grow + change

Help us not to fear the challenges but step out as Jesus says "Come"

Lecture Leaders Session 2 — Matthew Part 2

To Glory through the Cross

Matthew 16–17

Preparing for the Session

Central Focus

The First Commandment, "You shall have no other gods before Me," is more easily recited than lived. This session examines discipleship as self-denial and suffering with the hope of glory.

Objectives

That the participant, as a child of God and with the Holy Spirit's help, will be led to

1. understand the true nature of Israel's Messiah;
2. feel overwhelmed but all the more called to a life of self-denial;
3. leave glory to the future and fill the present with the concern of discipleship.

Note for small-group leaders: Lesson notes and other materials you will need begin on page 65.

For the Lecture Leader

Two sections of the biblical text are of critical importance this week. In 16:21–28 Jesus predicts His death and resurrection and bids us carry the cross. As you prepare for the lecture, meditate on this text's meaning for your own daily life. Is Jesus a part of your daily life? Our answer by God's grace can be "No, He is my whole life."

Matthew 17:1–13, the story of the transfiguration, puts the cross and the glory into proper perspective for the Christian.

There are two difficult passages this week, 16:18 and 16:28. Be prepared to answer questions group members bring.

Finally, 16:19, the binding and loosing of sin, will be treated next week when we study 18:18. The biblical message this week is very challenging to us disciples. Lose yourself as you let the challenge draw you closer to Christ!

Session Plan

Worship

Recruit one of the participants to read aloud the prayer from this week's study leaflet. Then sing the hymn printed in the study leaflet. Note that accompaniment for the hymn can be found on the music CD that accompanies this course. If you plan to use it, find it on the disk and cue it up ahead of time.

Devotion

Suppose someone today did and said what Jesus of Nazareth did and said. Before long, CNN would have several researchers digging into His background. NBC would assign a reporter to tail Him. The tabloids, and soon the mainstream press, would demand answers. Where did He come from? Where did He get His authority?

This week's lesson dug into questions like those. As we zero in on Simon Peter's words in 16:16, we see that his one sentence speaks volumes in answer to our questions. Jesus is, first of all, *the Christ*.

Christ is a title, synonymous with *Messiah,* the *Anointed One.* The Christ came from the Father, filled with the power of the Father's Spirit to do His will (Psalm 45:7). Christ is the Holy One to whom all the prophets pointed and for whose coming all the saints longed.

Second, Jesus is the *Son*, the dearly beloved Son of the Father from all eternity. He is the "heir of all things" and the one "through whom [the Father] made the universe" as the writer of Hebrews tells us (Hebrews 1:2).

Finally, notice that Jesus is the Son of the *living* God

(16:16). The Old Testament often uses this description of the LORD to signify that He actively works for the good of His people. This "living God" is the God who "does stuff," who ultimately brought salvation to us through the sacrifice of His own Son, Jesus Christ.

Peter could not have known and believed any of this on his own. Neither can we. God Himself has revealed it to our hearts (16:17)! Let's thank Him for that revelation today.

Lecture Presentation

This lecture also appears on the CD-ROM that accompanies this course. Also look at the PDFFILES directory on the CD-ROM for overhead transparency graphics for the course.

Introduction: No Easy Romp

Discipleship is no easy romp down life's road. Following Christ can fill us with joy, but it also makes challenges and burdens certain.

1 Our Blessed Confession

You and I know we are following the Christ. Jesus was not John the Baptizer or Elijah or Jeremiah or one of the prophets. He is not just a great preacher or a charismatic leader of the past. He is the Son of God, begotten of the Father and come into the world for us and for our salvation. With Peter (16:16) we say, "You are the Christ, the Son of the living God." This is a blessed confession (16:17): "Blessed are you, Simon son of Jonah, for this was not revealed to you by man, but by My Father in heaven." Upon this confession Jesus builds His church. This is the rock (16:18) that cannot be overcome, even by hell itself.

It would be great to stop here, in the sunshine of this declaration. But Jesus keeps going. He bids us follow further. He teaches us what our blessed confession really means. First (16:21), it meant that His own life was not to be a carefree romp into a glorious kingdom: "Jesus began to explain to His disciples that He must go to Jerusalem and suffer many things at the hands of the elders, chief priests and teachers of the law, and that He must be killed and on the third day be raised to life."

I can't overemphasize the importance of this "passion prediction." Twice in this week's lesson and later in 20:17–19, Jesus tells His disciples what is going to happen. He tells them about both the cross and the empty tomb, words on which they could have rested their faith in the trying times ahead. Later, after the crucifixion and resurrection, the disciples were reminded of these predictions (28:6; Luke 24:26).

The disciples didn't listen—probably because they didn't want to hear. Truth be told, we don't like to hear about the trouble and heartache that will result from our connection to Christ either. In this week's text we've run into some hard truths. Even so, we can take comfort in them. Jesus knew about His suffering and death ahead of time. He went through with it anyway. That's how deep His love for us is! He also tells us we will encounter hardships. That assures us that nothing that happens to us takes Him by surprise. In love, He will see us through all troubles, strengthen us in them, and finally, take us safely to Himself in heaven. Knowing that, we can face the truth He tells us—even when we'd rather not hear it.

2 Messianic Expectations

Jesus' own life was no carefree romp to glory. And just as Peter's confession had a special meaning for Jesus' ministry, so too our confession of faith comes with a price tag attached. Only moments after Peter's blessed confession, Peter and Jesus exchange sharp words (16:22–23): "Peter took Him aside and began to rebuke Him. 'Never, Lord!' he said. 'This shall never happen to you!' Jesus turned and said to Peter, 'Get behind Me, Satan! You are a stumbling block to Me; you do not have in mind the things of God, but the things of men.'"

This exchange shows that Peter, like many Jews of the day, did not expect a Messiah who would suffer. Understanding the difference between what they expected and what they got will teach us what our confession "You are the Christ" really means.

Display visual 2A from the CD-ROM.

What were Peter and the Jews of that day expecting? We have sufficient biblical and extrabiblical literature to answer that question. Rather than suffering and death, they eagerly anticipated a glorious earthly kingdom in which God would visibly vindicate Israel and exalt His people in Israel for all the world to see. Several New Testament passages reveal this. For instance:

> In Matthew 20:20–28 the mother of James and John, Zebedee's sons, knelt before Jesus to ask a favor. Matthew 20:21—"Grant that one of these two sons of mine may sit at Your right and the other at Your left in Your kingdom."

> In Luke 9:54 the disciples are ready to be vindicated before the Samaritans: "Lord, do You want us to call fire down from heaven to destroy them?"

> In Acts 1:6, just before Christ's ascension, the disciples asked, "Lord, are You at this time going to restore the kingdom to Israel?"

Besides Bible passages, we have a collection of nonbiblical poems called the Psalms of Solomon, written in the first century before Christ. Listen to their description of the glorious messianic king and His kingdom.

> *Behold, O Lord, and raise up unto them their king, the son of David,*
> *At the time in which Thou seest, O God, that he may reign over Israel Thy servant.*
> *And gird him with strength, that he may shatter unrighteous rulers,*
> *And that he may purge Jerusalem from nations that trample (her) down to destruction.*
> *Wisely, righteously, he shall thrust out sinners from (the) inheritance. ...*
> *He will rebuke rulers, and remove sinners by the might of his word;*
> *And (relying) upon his God, throughout his days he will not stumble;*
> *For God will make him mighty by means of (His) holy spirit. ...*
> *And the blessing of the Lord (will be) with him: he will be strong and stumble not;*
> *His hope (will be) in the Lord: who then can prevail against him?*

Psalm of Solomon 17:23–26, 42–44. R.H. Charles, ed., *The Apocrypha and Pseudepigrapha of the Old Testament in English*, vol. 2, (Oxford: Oxford University Press, 1913).

3 Christ Must Suffer

That's the Messiah Israel expected. No stumbling. No one will prevail against him. No wonder Peter and so many others were shocked by the Messiah they got. Suffering and death did not fit the credentials of the Messiah they had been waiting for. Not at all! That's why (16:22) Peter rebuked Jesus' description of His coming death. In reply (16:23) the Lord called Peter Satan, a stumbling block, one whose thoughts ran in a direction opposite those of God. Our Lord made it crystal clear: "The way that Israel's Messiah is going to travel is the road to Jerusalem, a road that will not end in the glorious kingdom of human fancy but in the cross and in the empty tomb."

Before we go further—and further means that we followers of Jesus must also suffer—we must understand why. With two diametrically opposed views of the Messiah, why is Jesus' definition of the Messiah's work correct and Peter's wrong? Of course, an easy and proper answer is, "Because Jesus and the Bible say so." The Bible not only gives us proof texts, it also explains the reason the Messiah had to suffer and die. Please follow as I move along step-by-step:

> God is holy; we are sinners.

> God is also just, and His divine justice must be satisfied.

> Therefore, sin must be punished.

> Who is punished by the divine justice? The sinner, of course. That's you and me.

> Still, God loves us. He doesn't want us to suffer, cut off from His presence for all eternity.

> God made a way out of this hellish predicament; He found a substitute, a substitute able to endure God's wrath at our sin.

> Hence Jesus, who comes as our Messiah, our Savior, must suffer our punishment in our place.

Display visual 2B from the CD-ROM.

Must. Underline that word in 16:21! "Jesus began to explain to His disciples that He must go to Jerusalem and suffer many things at the hands of the elders, chief priests and teachers of the law, and that He must be killed and on the third day be raised to life" (16:21). This same word occurs in the parallel texts of Mark and Luke. Peter learned that the true Messiah must of necessity suffer. On Pentecost he said (Acts 2:23): "This man was handed over to you by God's set purpose and foreknowledge; and you, with the help of wicked men, put Him to death by nailing Him to the cross." Peter preached that this necessary, preordained suffering brought the forgiveness of sins (Acts 2:38): "Repent and be baptized, every one of you, in the name of Jesus Christ for the forgiveness of your sins." Peter and many other Jews had expected the Messiah to glorify earthly Israel. Not so! What they got, what we have, is the Messiah we must have, a Messiah whose suffering makes us righteous before God.

4 Your Cross

Thomas Sheppard wrote this verse:

> Must Jesus bear His cross alone
> And all the world go free?
> No, there's a cross for everyone
> And there's a cross for me!

The cross that we are to carry is not for the forgiveness of our sins. Jesus carried that cross. What then is the cross? List the burdens you are carrying. Arthritis? Poverty? Family problems? Career failure? Such problems are sometimes called crosses, but this is not what Jesus means when He says (16:24-25): "If anyone would come after Me, he must deny himself and take up his cross and follow Me. For whoever wants to save his life will lose it, but whoever loses his life for Me will find it."

Display visual 2C from the CD-ROM.

The cross He bids you carry is to forget about yourself and live, work, play, think, speak, breathe only for Him. The first great commandment (22:37; Deuteronomy 6:5) says: "Love the Lord your God with all your heart and with all your soul and with all your mind." The "cross" is total discipleship. Seen this way, our worries over our own physical well-being may actually be a self-centered denial of our discipleship. To borrow Jesus'

earlier words to Peter, many of the things that worry us Christians are the things of men and not the things of God. God's thing is for you to deny yourself and follow Jesus.

Your eternal destiny is at stake. Jesus asks (16:26-27): "What good will it be for a man if he gains the whole world, yet forfeits his soul? Or what can a man give in exchange for his soul? For the Son of Man is going to come in His Father's glory with His angels, and then He will reward each person according to what he has done."

5 Sometime Glory; Present Listening

Discipleship is no easy romp down life's yellow brick road. Denying yourself so that (Acts 17:28) you might live and move and have your whole being in Christ means a life full of burdens. There are times when care-filled Christians would like to get out from under them. Hence the transfiguration, where God puts our care-filled life in the perspective of sometime glory and present listening.

Let me speak first about sometime glory. Glory is so alluring. When we Christians grow tired of denying ourselves, the divine glory looks especially attractive. Apparently spiritual people love to talk about glory. The old Gospel song says, "Visions of rapture now burst on my sight." Many Christians are fascinated, some obsessed, with Revelation and biblical prophecy. They study endlessly to find out more about the when and how of our entrance into heavenly glory. True, this study is legitimate—but only in its proper place. When Paul said that nothing in all creation will be able to separate us from the love of God that is in Christ Jesus our Lord (Romans 8:39), he specifically included angels, heights, and the future—the things of glory.

Jesus' transfiguration (17:1-13) makes the same point. On a mountain unknown to us (probably not the traditional Mount Tabor), Jesus' appearance was literally changed in front of Peter, James, and John. We read (17:2): "His face shone like the sun, and His clothes became as white as the light." Peter liked the divine glory he saw and was ready to settle in (17:4). "Lord, it is good for us to be here. If You wish, I will put up three shelters—one for You, one for Moses and one for Elijah." But Jesus ignores this offer. No shelters or shrines were to be, not at that point. Our dwelling in glory is reserved for sometime in the future. The glory on the mountain soon withdrew, and the disciples heard this command from the heavenly Father (17:5): "This is My Son, whom I love; with Him I am well pleased. Listen to Him!"

Sometime glory; present listening. While the disciples always remembered that awesome transfiguration, immediately afterward they began to listen to Christ. They listened to Him speak with Moses and Elijah about His death (Luke 9:30–31). They listened many more times to those passion predictions. They listened and heard Him say (16:24): "If anyone would come after Me, he must deny himself and take up his cross and follow Me."

Years later, Peter would write about that glory and that voice (2 Peter 1:16–19): "We were eyewitnesses of His majesty. For He received honor and glory from God the Father when the voice came to Him from the Majestic Glory, saying, 'This is My Son, whom I love; with Him I am well pleased.' We ourselves heard this voice that came from heaven when we were with Him on the sacred mountain. And we have the word of the prophets made more certain, and you will do well to pay attention to it, as to a light shining in a dark place."

Conclusion: Called to Suffer

That word of the prophets, centered on the Christ, invites us to life with Him. That life doesn't always work as smoothly as we would like. Sometimes obedience hurts. Sometimes discipleship exacts a higher price than we think we want to pay. And yet, when we fix our eyes on Jesus, we see the glory of His love for us. *That* glory belongs to us even now, whether we feel it or not. That infinite love—love that led our Savior all the way to Calvary—makes whatever burden we carry for Christ (11:29–30) easy and light, just as our Lord promised it would.

The apostle Paul, who knew a thing or two about carrying the cross of the Christian, wrote these words of encouragement in 2 Corinthians 4:16–18.

Therefore we do not lose heart. Though outwardly we are wasting away, yet inwardly we are being renewed day by day. For our light and momentary troubles are achieving for us an eternal glory that far outweighs them all. So we fix our eyes not on what is seen, but on what is unseen. For what is seen is temporary, but what is unseen is eternal.

Concluding Activities

Distribute study leaflet 3 and encourage participants to read the article "Making Disciples" on pages 10–11 of the enrichment magazine.

Notes

Helping Disciples Restore an Erring Brother

Matthew 18

Preparing for the Session

Central Focus

The quality of our life with God and with one another requires that we give careful attention to the welfare of one another's soul. The song that says "they are precious in His sight; Jesus loves the little children of the world" is true of all disciples. This session is about how we demonstrate it in our relationships with one another.

Objectives

That the participant, as a child of God and with the Holy Spirit's help, will be led to

1. take greater care not to cause others to sin;
2. gain a more accurate understanding of the steps for dealing with sin outlined in Matthew 18;
3. think of discipleship less as an individual pursuit and more as a group concern.

Note for small-group leaders: Lesson notes and other materials you will need begin on page 68.

For the Lecture Leader

The verses of Matthew 18 are probably familiar to you. Don't let that familiarity prevent you from scrutinizing the chapter as though you were looking at it for the first time. There is much here for the most seasoned Christian still to learn!

Three concepts used in the lecture may prove helpful in your study of the text: *imagination, common sense,* and *inspiration.* The Word of God, of course, remains normative, but these three can help you see how relevant that Word is for our Christian life.

About the delivery of the lecture—present the introduction slowly. This will give your listeners time to imagine they were someone else. That will help make them true participants in the lecture.

Session Plan

Worship

Find 10 volunteers to read one stanza each of the prayer found in this week's study leaflet. Then sing the hymn printed in the study leaflet. Note that accompaniment for the hymn can be found on the music CD that accompanies this course. If you plan to use it, find it on the disk and cue it up for easy use.

Devotion

A recent television documentary portrayed the emotional struggle of people who cut or burn themselves on purpose. This self-torture is hard to understand, difficult to treat. Even so, we can't help but feel enormous compassion for people who suffer in this way.

Yet, lest we think ourselves immune from such self-torture, we need to think more deeply about Jesus' parable in Matthew 18:21–35. Haven't we at times tortured ourselves by harboring unforgivingness in our hearts? Haven't we hit the rewind buttons of our minds in order to review again and again someone's insult, someone's harsh words or actions?

Our Lord was right. By not forgiving we place ourselves in the hands of the torturers. (See 18:34.) What key will open the door of our prison and release us to the "joy of [God's] salvation" (Psalm 51:12)? First, we need to recognize that our struggles with forgiveness are mere symptoms of a deeper problem—our failure to grasp the magnitude of our Lord's mercy to us. Beating ourselves up for harboring unforgivingness in our hearts won't change those hearts. We can only admit our weakness. We can only ask for His pardon and power.

The Good News is that He grants both in abundance. Deep change seldom happens overnight. But as we continually drink deeply from the river of grace that flows in His Word and in the Sacrament, we will find our attitudes transformed. We have His promise.

Lecture Presentation

This lecture also appears on the CD-ROM that accompanies this course. Also look at the PDFFILES directory on the CD-ROM for overhead transparency graphics for the course.

Introduction: Imagine You Were Someone Else

If you use your imagination, we'll get this lecture off to a good start. Imagine you were … that elderly person who moves ever so slowly. Imagine that's you, not someone else. Imagine you were … that shy high school youth with few friends and a poor self-image. Imagine that's you, not someone else. Imagine you were … hospitalized in a psychiatric ward, because life got to be too much for you to bear. That's you now, not someone else. Imagine you were … an older parent whose adult child has failed, perhaps at work, perhaps in marriage, perhaps in something else, but failed. That's not somebody else's child. It's yours. In short, imagine you were anybody but yourself. Put yourself in someone else's shoes. Assume all the thoughts, the fears, the hopes, the joys that person might have. Step out of yourself and into someone else's life.

This little exercise can make us sensitive to the precious nature of every single human life. You happen to be you. I happen to be me. That doesn't mean one of us is more important than the other, though we often act that way. Every human life is precious.

This observation is nothing uniquely Christian. It shows up in the secular world all the time. Newspapers have etiquette columns. Baseball fans hear appeals to be considerate of others. Robert's Rules of Order give everyone a chance at a meeting. You don't have to be a Christian to respect others.

What is uniquely Christian and what comes not from our imagination but from God's Word is the careful attention we disciples of Jesus Christ give to one another. We do this—or should—not simply because we are fellow human beings but because we are fellow believers following the same Savior to eternal glory. In Matthew 18 Jesus teaches us to attend most carefully to the discipleship of our fellow Christians. The last thing we want to do is trip up one of Christ's own.

1 Don't Trip 'Em Up

Don't trip 'em up. That's Jesus' warning to us in the first verses of Matthew 18. Don't trip up those people who, like you, are striving to follow Christ.

Display visual 3A from the CD-ROM.

The key concept here is "stumbling block," in Greek, *skandalon*. The word itself literally means a death trap or snare. For example, Psalm 141:9: "Keep me from the snares they have laid for me." The religious meaning of *skandalon* is a "temptation to sin, enticement to apostasy, false belief, etc." (*A Greek-English Lexicon of the New Testament and Other Early Christian Literature,* Bauer, Arndt, Gingrich, Danker). *Apostasy* means falling away from the faith. Jesus' concern in Matthew 18 is not about offensive social conduct. "I didn't like the tone of your voice." No, His concern is that you and I don't trip up our fellow believers and cause them to sin and fall from the faith.

Listen to what Jesus says in Matthew 18:6–9. (I'm reading from the New International Version, which translates *skandalon* as "causing [another] to sin.") "But if anyone causes one of these little ones who believe in Me to sin, it would be better for him to have a large millstone hung around his neck and to be drowned in the depths of the sea." (A millstone was a large, heavy, flat stone used for grinding grain; sometimes oxen hitched to this stone turned it as they walked around a mill.) "Woe to the world because of the things that cause people to sin! Such things [*skandalon* in the Greek text] must come, but woe to the man through whom they come!"

Note: This passage is not about children. It is about people of all ages who have a childlike faith. Elderly, adolescent, new Christians, doctors of theology—whatever the outward condition, Christ's sincere followers have a childlike faith. People of faith can be tripped up and tempted to sin—by us! Who among us knowingly wants to cause another to sin and fall from faith?

So, who is it that's hurt when parents fail to tell their children that so much of what they see on TV or on the Internet or in the movies is wrong? Who's hurt when a person claims to be as good a Christian as anybody else but only shows up at church on Christmas or Easter? Who's hurt when a group spends its time maligning an absent person? Who's hurt when Bible truths are forgotten in office politics or office parties? Who's hurt? It is that quiet Christian who notices the discrepancy between what Christians profess and what they do. That discrepancy easily trips up a childlike faith. It easily snares that Christian into sinful conduct. "Must be okay. Everybody's doing it!" Sin leads away from Christ and away from saving faith. So, woe to me and woe to you when our conduct or conversation causes a fellow Christian to fall into sin. It would be better to have a millstone hung around our neck and be drowned in the depths of the sea. Strong words!

Why so powerful an image? Because the immortal soul is so precious! It's one thing to imagine being in someone else's shoes. It's far different—and far more sobering—to jeopardize someone's eternal welfare, your own included! Matthew 18:8–9: "If your hand or your foot causes you to sin, cut it off and throw it away. It is better for you to enter life maimed or crippled than to have two hands or two feet and be thrown into eternal fire. And if your eye causes you to sin, gouge it out and throw it away. It is better for you to enter life with one eye than to have two eyes and be thrown into the fire of hell."

Eyes, hands, feet—our whole being—should aid discipleship. However, if what the eyes choose to see and the limbs choose to do weakens faith, you'd be better off without them. Is this an extreme statement? Yes, but you heard it first in the Sermon on the Mount (5:29–30). Our Lord makes the point forcefully: The eternal salvation of an immortal soul is a precious thing. John Calvin wrote, "It is no light matter to despise those who have angels for their companions and friends" (*Commentary on A Harmony to the Evangelists Matthew, Mark, and Luke*).

2 "Matthew 18"

Now we enter part two of this lecture. That other Christian remains just as precious when he or she has fallen into sin. Here Jesus means a big sin against you. So far today we've talked about our actions that tempt another to sin. Now Jesus shifts our attention to a fellow Christian, the "brother," who has succumbed to flagrant, open sin and will wander away from saving faith unless restored by confession and forgiveness. In these familiar words of Matthew 18:15–17 the theme remains the same: That person's soul is precious and needs to be kept in the fellowship—even if he has sinned against you. "If your brother sins against you, go and show him his fault, just between the two of you. If he listens to you, you have won your brother over. But if he will not listen, take one or two others along, so that 'every matter may be established by the testimony of two or three witnesses.' If he refuses to listen to them, tell it to the church; and if he refuses to listen even to the church, treat him as you would a pagan or a tax collector."

This is a famous text among church people. Just say "Matthew 18" in some groups and the conversation quickly shuts down. It's a great text, but it is also a greatly abused text. Let me make four points.

Display visuals 3B–3E from the CD-ROM as you work through the following points.

First, if your fellow Christian has sinned against you in an obvious way, keep the matter as quiet as possible. Jesus says (18:15): "If your brother sins against you, go and show him his fault, just between the two of you." If that fails, Jesus says, bring one or two witnesses. Don't bring in the whole militia. Don't announce your intentions over coffee at the office. Keep the matter as quiet as possible. Why? It is of utmost importance that the sinner be restored and be able to continue in the fellowship. If the sin is broadcast throughout the congregation, the sinner may repent but still be too embarrassed to maintain active fellowship with the congregation. Imagine how you would feel if everybody knew about the skeletons in your closet—skeletons confessed and skeletons forgiven, but skeletons nonetheless. You would probably be too ashamed to continue your discipleship with that group of Christians. Because the soul of this sinning Christian is so precious, Jesus advises you to keep the sin as quiet as possible.

Second, Jesus is talking about flagrant, open sin—sin that has without question occurred and has been committed by a "brother," another believer. This is proven by verse 16, where Jesus quotes Deuteronomy 19:15 when He says, "If he will not listen, take one or two others along, so that 'every matter may be established by the testimony of two or three witnesses.'"

Now we don't need imagination; we just need plain ol' common sense. If you are going to take one or two people to help you talk to your Christian brother, the act you believe he has committed must be sinful and hurtful to that person or to your relationship with him. For example: If a fellow Christian lacks tact (in your opinion, that is), does Matthew 18 authorize you to reform him? Obviously not. But suppose the brother has said something that hurt your feelings. Should you tell him, according to Matthew 18?

Maybe. We are all sinners. Foibles and failings will mark our lives until we enter glory. Most of these sins do not come under the rubric of Matthew 18, but instead under 1 Peter 4:8: "Love covers over a multitude of sins." Where it's possible to overlook a fault, where the offense won't build a wall of suspicion and hurt between you and your brother, overlook it. Remember, you're a sinner too. On the other hand, Jesus wants us to be at peace with one another. He wants us to enjoy loving one another. That's where Matthew 18 comes in. But this truth appears throughout the New Testament. James 5:16 says, "Confess your sins to each other." In Galatians 6:1-2, St. Paul gives us a good summary: "Brothers, if someone is caught in a sin, you who are spiritual should restore him gently. But watch yourself, or you also may be tempted. Carry each other's burdens, and in this way you will fulfill the law of Christ."

Third, when all fails and the matter is referred to the church, the church's concern is always the restoration of the sinner. That means that even if the repeated pleas of the church go unheeded and the sinner is removed from the fellowship, our goal always remains restoration. Jesus says (18:17): "If he refuses to listen even to the church, treat him as you would a pagan or a tax collector." What kind of treatment is that to be? The unrepentant sinner is outside the fellowship, just as tax collectors and pagans were outside of Israel's fellowship. Yet this unrepentant sinner remains an object of the church's great concern. The model for this behavior is Jesus, who once quoted His opponents' criticisms of Him (11:19): "The Son of Man came eating and drinking, and they say, 'Here is a glutton and a drunkard, a friend of tax collectors and "sinners".'" Jesus befriends sinners. Jesus always cares deeply about sinners. The soul of the unrepentant sinner remains precious! Like the Good Shepherd we worship, the church should always have a heart willing to leave the 99 to go seek the one that is lost. As Jesus says (18:14): "Your Father in heaven is not willing that any of these little ones should be lost."

Finally, in all efforts to restore the brother, you can rest assured that Jesus, the Son of the heavenly Father, will be present (vv. 18-20). "I tell you the truth, whatever you bind on earth will be bound in heaven, and whatever you loose on earth will be loosed in heaven. Again, I tell you that if two of you on earth agree about anything you ask for, it will be done for you by My Father in heaven. For where two or three come together in My name, there am I with them."

In these words Jesus gives us much more than a general blessing upon any gathering of Christians. Specifically, He promises to be present in our efforts to restore an unrepentant sinner. This is not just an assurance that He will be present at a Bible study or church picnic. Those are not crises. Rather, taken in context, these verses provide comfort and strength for those tough times when you have to talk with someone about what they have done wrong. Doesn't the thought of confronting someone about sin make you nervous? Jesus promises to be there with you, a full partner in the effort to restore the fallen sinner and regain that precious soul.

Conclusion: Inspiration for Us All

To do that requires inspiration. We started this lecture by imagining what it would be like to be someone else. Matthew 18 has taken us much further. Our life as followers of Jesus Christ is not simply a matter of respecting others, but instead caring for their life of faith. For that we need inspiration, inspiration not to trip up a fellow believer and cause him to sin. Should he sin against us, we need inspiration to restore him.

Peter, too, sensed the enormity of this task. How long can we do this, he wondered. Jesus' answer was 70 times 7, or, according to some manuscripts, 77 times. Take your pick. Either way, it's a lifetime of caring for precious souls. Remember that the number 7 in the culture of that day represented completion or totality. So 77 or 70 times 7 extended forgiveness to cover all offenses our brothers and sisters in the faith commit.

The power to live this life is our remembrance—our remembrance as a group, not merely as individuals—our remembrance of the heavenly Father's mercy toward us in canceling our debt of sin. The parable of the unmerciful servant, which concludes this week's lesson (18:23–35), is Jesus' reminder that our discipleship is a result of divine mercy. To forgive or not to forgive is God's prerogative, not ours. Since He has forgiven, any failure on our part to forgive one another upsets the whole body of believers. Listen to verse 31. "When the other servants saw what had happened, they were greatly distressed." The Father's mercy, which we have so freely received, makes us servants who want to share divine mercy with one another. We Christians don't need to imagine being someone else. We only need to know that together we are His.

Please join me in this prayer: *Almighty God, by Your Holy Spirit You have made us one with Your saints in heaven and on earth. Grant that in our earthly pilgrimage we may always be supported by this fellowship of love and prayer and know ourselves to be surrounded by their witness to Your power and mercy. We ask this for the sake of Jesus Christ, in whom all our intercessions are acceptable through the Spirit, and who lives and reigns forever and ever. Amen.*

Concluding Activities

Distribute study leaflet 4 and encourage participants to read the article "The Keys to the Kingdom" on pages 14–16 of the enrichment magazine.

Notes

Lecture Leaders Session 4 — Matthew Part 2

Preparing Disciples to Trust in God's Grace

Matthew 19–20

Preparing for the Session

Central Focus

Childlike trust in God and service to others are the qualities of following Christ. This session brings those virtues home against the backdrop of calculating self-interest.

Objectives

That the participant, as a child of God and with the Holy Spirit's help, will be led to

1. ask for God to grant childlike trust in Christ;
2. learn to abhor egotistical self-interest;
3. act in Christlike and childlike ways in all relationships;
4. be awed by God's grace.

Note for small-group leaders: Lesson notes and other materials you will need begin on page 71.

For the Lecture Leader

Two images thread their way through this lecture: the trust of a child and a serpent in the bosom. The first is readily understood, but why the second? The image of a serpent in the bosom comes from Nathaniel Hawthorne's short story "Egotism; or, The Bosom Serpent." You may be intrigued enough to read the story, though it is not necessary for lecture purposes. The image is repulsive. When you're done with the lecture, the students should be equally repulsed by self-seeking conduct. Much more appealing is the simplicity of a child!

Please give careful thought to what the lecture says about marriage and divorce. We easily become legalists, asking questions about what is permitted and what is forbidden. Far more helpful to in-depth study is to ask *why* some things are permitted and others forbidden. Careful thought given to the Bible text will give clearer understanding to questions of marriage and divorce, important in this day and age.

As you study these chapters (for that matter, any biblical texts), note that some verbs are active and others passive. Note, for example, Matthew 19:29; 20:23. The distinction between active and passive will help you understand the lecture's conclusion on grace.

Finally, as has been said before, set aside ample time to meditate word for word upon the scriptural text. The Holy Spirit has included countless precious truths in these texts. He has put the words together in just this way for a purpose. Meditate on them!

Session Plan

Worship

As you begin, invoke God's presence by saying, "In the name of God the Father, who created us; in the name of God the Son, who redeemed us; and in the name of God the Holy Spirit, who calls and strengthens us through God's Word. Amen." Then sing the hymn printed in the study leaflet. Close this brief time of worship by asking one of the participants to read aloud the prayer in the study leaflet.

Devotion

Suppose the company you work for decided to give bonuses at the end of the fiscal year—two weeks from now. Would you be excited to hear this news? Suppose your bonus as a long-term employee was $1,500. Would you still feel excited? Now suppose the person in the cubicle next to yours will also receive $1,500, and she was just hired last week! Are you still excited? Or are you a bit disgusted or even angry?

If we understand the parable of 20:1–16 as talking

about fairness, we won't ever understand it. If we think that God's kingdom is about fairness, we miss out on much joy.

Jesus' parable, you see, says a lot about meaning, about life's true purpose. Think about the workers described in 20:6–7. All day long, they have twiddled their thumbs. No one hired them. Anyone who's ever looked for work knows about the boredom, the worry, the feelings of uselessness, rejection, and even despair involved in unemployment. Few who have lived through it want to go back.

Contrast this with the situation of the workers in 20:1–2. They have the security of a paycheck and the satisfaction of a meaningful, productive day. But their words (20:12) betray their hearts. They've been slaving in resentment instead of enjoying their blessings.

How is it with you? As you recognize the blessing of peace with God in Jesus' cross, do you enjoy the security and peace He so freely gives? Do you take advantage of opportunities to add meaning to life by serving Him? Or do you resent others who come to these joys late in life? What will you say to your Lord about all this right now?

(Allow for a few moments of silent prayer. Then offer a prayer from your own heart thanking Jesus for the meaning, purpose, and pardon His cross has brought into our lives.)

Lecture Presentation

This lecture also appears on the CD-ROM that accompanies this course. Also look at the PDFFILES directory on the CD-ROM for overhead transparency graphics for the course.

Introduction: Childlike Trust in Jesus

A pastor, driving home with his wife, overheard his daughters talking in the back seat. The younger daughter, a first grader, asked her older sister how a dead person could be in heaven and at the funeral home at the same time. The pastor joined the conversation and answered the question. Or so he thought. After several moments of silence, the first grader said, "I think I'll ask my teacher."

Simple trust like that of this first grader in her teacher lies behind Jesus' words (19:14): "Let the little children come to Me, and do not hinder them, for the kingdom of heaven belongs to such as these." Small children are transparently honest, unlearned in the adult world's cunning and self-seeking ways. Chapters 19 and 20 of Matthew present the conflict between self-interest and the ideal of discipleship: childlike simplicity that trusts God and serves others with no thought of personal gain. That is the lesson we want to learn now from Jesus our teacher.

1 Not to Be Served, but to Serve

Our Lord teaches us, His children, to serve others by serving us. That's the way He did it. What's more, His service empowers ours. Your studies this past week brought you to Christ's third prediction of His passion (Matthew 20:17–19). Like the first two passion predictions, Jesus lays this one out in clear, straightforward words: "We are going up to Jerusalem, and the Son of Man will be betrayed to the chief priests and the teachers of the law. They will condemn Him to death and will turn Him over to the Gentiles to be mocked and flogged and crucified. On the third day He will be raised to life!"

Shortly after this prediction Jesus reiterated the purpose of His life and then stated His purpose for our lives: to serve others. In 20:26–28 He says, "Whoever wants to become great among you must be your servant, and whoever wants to be first must be your slave—just as the Son of Man did not come to be served, but to serve, and to give His life as a ransom for many."

Display visual 4A from the CD-ROM.

Though the word *ransom* is used only here in the New Testament, Jewish listeners would have understood Jesus' meaning immediately. The Old Testament accented the idea of ransom over and over again. In Numbers 3:12 God sets the Levites aside to serve Him full-time in place of every firstborn Israelite male. Exodus 21:30 presents another instance of the idea: "If payment is demanded of him, he may redeem his life by paying whatever is demanded." The prophet Hosea married a prostitute who ran away from home and ended up as a slave. Hosea bought her back—ransomed her—and took her home again as his wife. Chiefly, though, the entire system of sacrifice enacted the idea of ransom. The lamb lost its life in place of the sinner while the sinner went free. Goats, rams, bulls—all the animals that died on the altars of the tabernacle and the temple preached silent sermons about ransom. So when Jesus tells His followers (20:26–28) that He came "to give His life as a ransom," He was not introducing some strange, new concept.

2 Egotism; or, The Bosom Serpent

Too often, though, simple service to others strikes us as a strange, new concept. Jesus teaches us to be servants, yes, even slaves. Here's where the simple life of discipleship gets more complicated. Little children, like that first grader who had a simple trust in her teacher, get older and more acquainted with the self-centered ways of the adult world. In similar fashion, we adult disciples believe in Jesus but have also been exposed to the self-seeking ways of the world. So, when we hear simple words from our Teacher about being servants and slaves, we can come up with some pretty plausible excuses to avoid opportunities for service.

Nathaniel Hawthorne, a 19th-century author from New England, wrote a short story entitled "Egotism; or, The Bosom Serpent." It is the story of a man named Roderick Elliston, who was obsessed with himself. He was so obsessed that he had, or thought he had, a snake in his bosom. When you read the story you find yourself wondering if there really was a serpent in his bosom. Roderick Elliston's constant complaint about this egotistical serpent was, "It gnaws me! It gnaws me!" It's a repulsive image, to be sure. But keep it in mind as we look at Matthew 19–20.

It gnaws at people today—sometimes even Christian people—to treat marriage as a lifelong commitment. Self-interest, like a serpent, can slither into a marriage and destroy this good gift from God. For example, think about the Pharisees' question (19:3): "Is it lawful for a man to divorce his wife for any and every reason?" Surely self-interest lay behind this request. Perhaps someone's marriage had become inconvenient. Maybe someone's wife had become chronically ill or just hard to live with. The Pharisees trotted out a Bible passage to bolster their claim to independence. Deuteronomy 24:1 says, "If a man marries a woman who becomes displeasing to him because he finds something indecent about her, and he writes her a certificate of divorce, gives it to her and sends her from his house …" Misusing Scripture (if you don't think so, read the text in context), the Pharisees had transformed the divine and insoluble marriage bond into a kind of human Velcro. When self-interest indicates it, you can undo marriage as easily as if you were loosening a Velcro strap on your shoe.

Jesus calls that hardness of heart. In marriage the Creator—not the man or woman—makes the couple one. The two become one. One in the act of love. One in the procreation of children. But also one in a mystical sense that demonstrates Christ's love for His bride, the church. Jesus met the Pharisees' misuse of Scripture by appealing to Genesis 2:24: "For this reason a man will leave his father and mother and be united to his wife, and they will become one flesh." This is the way it should be. Little children know that divorce is wrong and that it hurts, no matter how thoroughly Mommy and Daddy try to explain it to them. We adult disciples need to see that self-interest gnaws at us and can destroy the divine unity God intends for marriage.

Even so, our Lord makes one exception. In 19:9 Jesus says, "I tell you that anyone who divorces his wife, except for marital unfaithfulness, and marries another woman commits adultery." This verse speaks of improper conduct—the committing of adultery ("except for marital unfaithfulness"). Jesus also condemns divorcing a faithful partner to marry another ("Anyone who divorces his wife … and marries another woman"). In either case—and here's the point—one marriage partner has acted independently and severed the divine marriage bond. Jesus says that is not to be (19:6): "What God has joined together, let man not separate." When husband or wife turns the marriage bonds into Velcro by committing adultery, Jesus allows divorce. Other Scriptures elaborate on this.

Display visual 4B from the CD-ROM.

Scripture indicates that only three things break the marriage bond—death (Romans 7:2), adultery (Matthew

19:9), or the desertion of a faithful Christian by an unbelieving spouse (1 Corinthians 7:15). Note two things here. First, Jesus' words and Paul's words—God's Word—apply to *Christians*. We cannot expect unbelievers to understand or live according to them. Would it be best for society? Yes. But attempts to make laws regulating divorce this strictly have largely failed.

Second, the application of these teachings calls for special care. The potential for lasting damage is so great. We cannot always look at the lives of our brothers or sisters from the outside and know what's going on. While Scripture sets a very high standard for issues of marriage and divorce, Christians do not worship marriage as an idol. In cases of physical abuse, sexual violence, and some other instances as well, the offending party has "deserted" the spouse, whether or not the two still live together under the same roof.

Have Christians, even some Christian leaders, taken the issue of divorce too lightly in the past? Possibly. But that fact will not justify smug self-righteousness in our own hearts as we look around at the families in our congregation. Jesus' attitude toward sin should be our own—grief at the pain sin causes and a heart that yearns to help, to confront when necessary, and to restore the sinner. Last week's text—Matthew 18—was tailor-made for just such situations.

To summarize, instead of a gnawing self-centered view of our role in our marriage, God wants husband and wife to serve one another "just as the Son of Man did not come to be served, but to serve, and to give His life as a ransom for many" (20:28). St. Paul says the same thing. Speaking to husbands, he says that marriage is an occasion for Christlike service. Ephesians 5:25–28: "Husbands, love your wives, just as Christ loved the church and gave Himself up for her to make her holy, cleansing her by the washing with water though the word, and to present her to Himself as a radiant church, without stain or wrinkle or any other blemish, but holy and blameless. In this same way, husbands ought to love their wives."

God help us use our marriage as a daily occasion for Christlike, childlike service!

"It gnaws me! It gnaws me!" cried Roderick Elliston.

Simple faith and service are also sorely tried by issues of money. How would you feel if someone told you, "Sell your possessions and give to the poor, and you will have treasure in heaven. Then come, follow Me"? Was the rich young man who first heard those words—19:21—a miser? a Scrooge? Maybe not. But regardless, Jesus' words were too much. Verse 22 tells us, "When the young man heard this, he went away sad, because he had great wealth."

Much like the Pharisees, this young man had elevated the self-interests of the creature—himself—above the divine will of the Creator. The young man was more devoted to his material wealth than to God. He thought he could satisfy the second table of the Law (Commandments 4–10), even though his own material self-interest was his real "god" in violation of the First Commandment. He claimed (19:18–19) that he had kept the commandments: " 'Do not murder, do not commit adultery, do not steal, do not give false testimony, honor your father and mother,' and 'love your neighbor as yourself.' " But Jesus zeroed in on his root sin—the young man loved himself more than God. Service to others that came from simple faith in Christ proved too much for this young man to handle.

Does this egotistical serpent ever gnaw you? Would you abandon the dearest things in your life to demonstrate your childlike devotion to Jesus? If we're honest, we must confess that we see evidence that the egotistical serpent has slithered into our lives. Money and possessions seem to provide such a good backup in case God doesn't come through for us. The snake is there, even in us Christian people.

3 The Serpent Crushed

Yes, but his head has been crushed. When Adam and Eve followed their own selfish hearts instead of obeying God's Word, God gave this promise (Genesis 3:15): "I will put enmity between you and the woman, and between your offspring and hers; He will crush your head, and you will strike His heel." That first promise of the Savior was fulfilled at the cross. Satan, who struck at the heel of Christ, found his dominion crushed by Christ's death. In that death Jesus gave His life as a ransom for many. In Jesus' resurrection and ascension (Ephesians 1:20–22), God "raised Him from the dead and seated Him at His right hand in the heavenly realms, far above all rule and authority, power and dominion. … And God placed all things under His feet."

The dominion of the egotistical serpent has been crushed. We can be rid of it in our lives. We can serve one another with a Christlike and childlike trust. All we need is to hear again and again the lesson of our Teacher. Did you notice this past week that the disciples were stunned by what Jesus said about marriage (Matthew 19:10)? "If this is the situation between a husband and wife, it is better not to marry." They were amazed again after Jesus' discussion with the rich young man (19:25): "Who then can be saved?" The disciples were starting to grow more childlike. They asked their teacher! And what does the Teacher say? "Children, it is grace. It is God's doing, not ours." To quote Jesus directly, He says of chastity and marriage (19:11): "Not everyone can accept this word, but only those to whom it has been given." To the disciples' perplexity about possessions and salvation, Jesus responds (19:26): "With man this is impossible, but with God all things are possible." That egotistical serpent may scowl fierce as he will, one word from our Teacher can fell him!

4 Grace Through and Through

Our final passage today is the parable of the workers in the vineyard (20:1–16). This parable elevates grace for us. It teaches us that simple childlike service is a gift of grace, not an act of service based on a self-centered hope of reward. Peter had reward on his mind when he said (19:27): "We have left everything to follow You! What then will there be for us?" The mother of Zebedee's sons wanted a reward for her boys (20:21): "Grant that one of these two sons of mine may sit at Your right and the other at Your left in Your kingdom." Don't we, too, sometimes wonder "What's in it for us?" Jesus tells us, as He told Peter, we will enjoy an eternal reward (19:28–29): "I tell you the truth, at the renewal of all things, when the Son of Man sits on His glorious throne, you who have followed Me will also sit on twelve thrones, judging the twelve tribes of Israel. And everyone who has left houses or brothers or sisters or father or mother or children or fields for My sake will receive a hundred times as much and will inherit eternal life."

Eternal rewards, Jesus told Zebedee's sons, are gifts of the Father (20:23): "These places belong to those for whom they have been prepared by My Father." Before that happens, there will be suffering (20:22–23): " 'Can you drink the cup I am going to drink?' 'We can,' they answered. Jesus said to them, 'You will indeed drink from My cup.' " The cup refers to His passion. The crosses and the cups, the renunciation of self-interest and Christlike service to others—we don't do these things to earn eternal rewards. Both earthly discipleship and heavenly glory come to us by God's grace through and through.

This is why we close with the parable of the workers in the vineyard (20:1–16). The story may have confused you at first. Why should those (20:12) who worked only an hour receive a full day's wage? Based on merit pay and human rules of fairness, the owner of the vineyard acted unjustly indeed. The world thinks that way, but it is not our Teacher's final lesson. God's final lesson is grace. If you have been blessed with years of faithful marriage; if you have been blessed with years of devotion to Jesus; if you have been a servant, even a slave for others—it's all grace. It is God's grace working in you the joy and satisfaction you receive through the years, just as it is grace that saves the sinner late in life.

Conclusion: "With God All Things Are Possible"

A visitor asked Roderick Elliston if there were any remedy for that awful egotistical serpent in the bosom.

"Yes, but an impossible one," muttered Roderick as he lay wallowing with his face in the grass. "Could I for one moment forget myself, the serpent might not abide within me. It is my diseased self-contemplation that has engendered and nourished him."

"Then forget yourself, my husband," said a gentle voice above him; "forget yourself in the idea of another!"

These were the words of his wife, Rosina, from whom he had been separated for four years.

She touched Roderick with her hand. A tremor shivered through his frame … Roderick Elliston sat up like a man renewed, restored to his right mind, and rescued from the fiend which had so miserably overcome him in the battle-field of his own breast.

Frederick C. Crews, ed., *Great Short Works of Nathaniel Hawthorne* (New York: Harper and Row, 1967).

The egotistical snake has gone. When he tries to come back into your life this week, "forget yourself in the idea of another." Remember Matthew 20:28, "The Son of Man did not come to be served, but to serve, and to give His life as a ransom for many." Matthew 19:26: "With God all things are possible."

Concluding Activities

Distribute study leaflet 5 and encourage participants to prepare for next week by reading "Faithful to Christ—And to Caesar" on pages 24–26 of the enrichment magazine.

Notes

Lecture Leaders Session 5   Matthew Part 2

The Disciples Learn to Talk about the Faith

Matthew 21–22

Preparing for the Session

Central Focus

The Large Catechism says, "The first things that issue and emerge from the heart are words" (LC I 50). Therefore, what is more natural for us disciples than talking about the Lord, the object of our faith? This lesson examines the words that Jesus spoke in His controversy with the religious leadership of Israel, words that teach us how to talk about our Lord and His salvation.

Objectives

That the participant, as a child of God and with the Holy Spirit's help, will be led to

1. talk about Jesus in everyday conversation;
2. understand that good works grow out of true faith;
3. produce good works through conversation;
4. center words of witness on faith in Jesus Christ.

Note for small-group leaders: Lesson notes and other materials you will need begin on page 75.

For the Lecture Leader

Words have power, especially when they paint a picture in the hearer's mind. Matthew 21–22 are filled with words that evoke pictures. Whether Matthew describes Jesus' dramatic actions or repeats the stories He tells, we can't help but see these chapters in our mind's eye. In this lesson's lecture we attempt to draw lessons from these pictures, lessons of faith and good works centered in Jesus Christ. These lessons teach us, in turn, to center our faith talk, our words of witness, in Christ. When we do that, the Holy Spirit uses the living and active Word of God to create and increase faith and good works. That's a picture we all want to see!

Chapters 21–22 climax in chapter 23, Jesus' pronouncement of woes upon the Pharisees and teachers of the law. You'll find it helpful to read all three chapters and, if preparation time permits, to scan the lecture for session 6. That lecture concentrates on the denunciation of the Pharisees and teachers of the law. Hence, the present lecture looks at Jesus' words about the failure of faith and fruits that led to His denunciation.

Session Plan

Worship

Begin the session by singing the hymn printed in the study leaflet. Use the music CD for accompaniment as needed. Then have two participants (arrange for this ahead of time) read the prayer—one (perhaps a man) to read the first section and the other (perhaps a woman) to read the second section.

Devotion

What was it like to know Jesus when He ministered here on earth? Imagine yourself as one of the Twelve who lived alongside Him. What overarching impressions present themselves?

Jesus saw. Jesus knew. Jesus acted in love. In essence, those three sentences form the outline for nearly all that Matthew reports in His Gospel. For instance, a few weeks ago we read that:

- Jesus saw the condition of the crowds (14:13; 15:32). Jesus knew they were hungry. Jesus acted in love to feed them, all of them—more than 5,000 in one group, more than 4,000 in the other.

- Jesus saw the disciples' struggle with the wind (14:24). Jesus knew they were tired and frustrated. Jesus came to them in love and spoke peace to their hearts.

And so it went. The crowds whose relatives lay fevered with disease. The lame, the mute, those whose bodies and whose spirits were broken by circumstances, mangled by accidents.

Jesus even saw the need of the Pharisees to be broken, to be drawn through repentance to true faith in the one, true Savior-God. In each case, Jesus knew. And Jesus acted in love to speak Law and to apply magnificent Gospel to the hearts of all who would turn to Him in repentance and faith. We saw our Lord respond to that need several times in this week's lesson.

What do you need today? Whatever that is, Jesus sees. Jesus knows. Jesus is ready to act in love. Ask Him.

Lecture Presentation

This lecture also appears on the CD-ROM that accompanies this course. Also look at the PDFFILES directory on the CD-ROM for overhead transparency graphics for the course.

Introduction: "We Don't Talk Religion"

"We don't talk religion or politics." Many people live out that motto. It's the motto of ostriches! Talking about the faith should come as as naturally for a disciple as talking is for any human being. Since our life is a journey with Christ, as we strive to follow Him in faith, it's only natural that this preoccupation shows up in our conversation. Yes, we do talk "religion" in this sense … and sometimes politics too.

You can hear the sharp words; you can feel the tension in the air as Jesus talks religion in chapters 21 and 22. He's not standing afar off, wagging His head, wringing His hands, and saying, "Isn't it a shame we can't all get along?" No, Jesus is right in there, deep in theological controversy. He rides into that controversy on a donkey, announcing to Jerusalem that He is the promised Messiah. He chases the money changers from the court of the Gentiles, so that His temple—God's temple—could be a place of prayer for all. He accepts the acclamations of the crowds that He is the Son of David and refuses to produce His credentials for the religious establishment, the chief priests and the teachers of the law. No wonder this week—Holy Week—turned out to be the greatest week in all of world history. What a start!

1 Dramatic Actions

On Monday Jesus zaps the fig tree. Just like the triumphal entry and the cleansing of the temple, Jesus does dramatic things to catch people's attention. That fig tree was there to produce fruit. Just so, God wants His people to produce the good works that come from faith. Perhaps you remember Matthew 7:16, 19: "By their fruit you will recognize them. … Every tree that does not bear good fruit is cut down and thrown into the fire." St. Paul lists some "fruit" in Galatians 5:22: "The fruit of the Spirit is love, joy, peace, patience, kindness, goodness, faithfulness, gentleness and self-control."

This fruit comes ultimately from God's revelation in His Son Jesus Christ: "Everything that I learned from My Father I have made known to you. You did not choose Me, but I chose you and appointed you to go and bear fruit—fruit that will last" (John 15:15–16). The religious leadership of Israel had not been producing that kind of fruit. So, early Monday morning on the way back to the city, He zaps the fig tree. It was a dramatic thing that set the stage for some words about faith.

We read in 21:21–22: "If you have faith and do not doubt, not only can you do what was done to the fig tree, but also you can say to this mountain, 'Go, throw yourself into the sea,' and it will be done. If you believe, you will receive whatever you ask for in prayer." You and I have no need to zap fig trees or to throw mountains into seas, but we do want an effective prayer life. The power of our prayers comes not from our zeal, not from our worthiness, but rather from the one to whom we pray. The power of prayer is the power of our Lord Jesus.

When we remember that, we can pray with confidence. We can focus on our Lord who always gives His children His best gifts. We need not beat ourselves up for "weak faith" when our Lord doesn't do what we think is best. Instead, we can rest in the knowledge that our Father answers His people's prayers in two ways. Either He says yes, and grants just what we have asked. Or He says, "I have something better for you." We may not see His answer as "better" right away. We may never see that answer as "better" while we live here on earth. But we can trust that the one who sent His Son to die for us will never give us any "second best" gifts.

As we think about Jesus' promise to hear and answer our prayers, we also remember that prayers of faith are not for selfish purposes; they are for God's purpose. We especially ask for the grace to produce fruit for Him. Although Jesus uses figurative language when He talks about moving mountains, He means what He says when He talks about God's faithful people who ask Him for the power to produce spiritual fruit (21:22): "If you believe, you will receive whatever you ask for in prayer."

2 Dramatic Words

This leads us into the three parables. When Jesus is not doing something dramatic, He weaves an action-filled story. Jesus' parables were effective audiovisuals before there were audiovisuals.

The parable of the two sons (21:28–32) presents true faith as penitent faith. Without such faith there can be no God-pleasing fruit (Hebrews 11:6). In verse 28 the father says, "Son, go and work today in the vineyard." The nation of Israel had often been compared to a vineyard in the Old Testament. For instance, Isaiah 5:7 says: "The vineyard of the LORD Almighty is the house of Israel, and the men of Judah are the garden of His delight. And He looked for justice, but saw bloodshed; for righteousness, but heard cries of distress." It's obvious Jesus is telling a story about the religious workers among His people. God expects fruit from penitent faith.

The son in 21:30 said he would go but didn't. That reminds us of Matthew 7:21: "Not everyone who says to Me, 'Lord, Lord,' will enter the kingdom of heaven, but only he who does the will of My Father who is in heaven." Israel's religious leadership did some fine religious talking, but their will was not lined up with God's (21:24–27, 32). That's why they rejected John the Baptizer's preaching of repentance.

The other son in the parable (21:29) is like the tax collectors and prostitutes who listened to John with repentant faith. The son who refused his father's request later changed his mind and went to do the father's will. This son reminds us of what Paul said to the Ephesians (2:8–10): "By grace you have been saved, through faith—and this not from yourselves, it is the gift of God—not by works, so that no one can boast. For we are God's workmanship, created in Christ Jesus to do good works, which God prepared in advance for us to do."

Jesus turns up the heat of the controversy by telling the parable of the tenants in 21:33–46. Here He tells the chief priests and Pharisees: "You are guilty of malfeasance in office. You have been warned repeatedly. You haven't changed. You are out." Can you imagine how tense the air must have been as Jesus said all this?

In 21:33 Jesus again uses the imagery of the vineyard from Isaiah 5. The chief priests and the Pharisees were supposed to labor on God's behalf among the people of Israel. Their labors, their ministries, were to produce fruit for *God's* glory, not their own. But they didn't do that. Not pleased to labor for their Father in His vineyard, they labored for themselves and abused their positions of trust.

Jesus continues in 21:34–39 by pointing out that they had heard many warnings. The landowner sent servants, and God sent the prophets. Jesus repeatedly demonstrates the fact that Israel's religious leadership rejected these messengers:

> 23:37—"O Jerusalem, Jerusalem, you who kill the prophets and stone those sent to you."

> 17:12—"I tell you, Elijah has already come, and they did not recognize him, but have done to him everything they wished."

> 5:12—"They persecuted the prophets who were before you."

Finally (21:37) the landowner sends his son, an obvious reference to Christ's coming (Hebrews 1:1–2). The landowner believes this will be decisive: "They will respect my son," he said. Though the tenants know they should respect the person of the son, they (21:38) willfully choose to reject him for their own selfish gain: "Come, let's kill him and take his inheritance." Needless to say, this didn't sit too well with the landowner or with God, who (21:43) will take the inheritance and give it to people who will produce fruit for Him. That leads us to Jesus' third parable, the wedding banquet.

Before getting into that story, let's pause and make application. When you talk about your faith, you need to remember who you are. You now are one of the tenants. You are one whom God has chosen to bear fruit for Him (John 15:16). In 21:41 we see the implied promise of the parable is that the landowner "will rent the vineyard to other tenants, who will give him his share of the crop at harvest time." This was fulfilled when the Lord entrusted His Gospel to the penitent believers of the Christian church and removed it from the religious leaders who presided over Jerusalem's temple. Your goal now is to produce fruit, especially to share with others the true Word of Christ by which the Holy Spirit creates both faith and its resultant fruit.

Dr. Martin Luther writes:

> *Until the last day the Holy Spirit remains with the holy community or Christian people. Through it he gathers us, using it to teach and preach the Word. By it he creates and increases sanctification, causing it daily to grow and become strong in the faith and in the fruits of the Spirit.*

LC II 53

One day each of us will render account for those fruits. As we speak, we can remember that we are now the tenants to whom God looks for the fruit produced by penitent faith. Then we will hear Jesus say one day (25:23): "Well done, good and faithful servant!"

This brings us to the third parable (22:1–14) and the content of our faith talk. Fruit comes from faith, and faith comes from the Word of Christ. Sooner or later when we talk about the faith, we must get to Jesus Christ. He is always the real focus of conversation.

The parable begins in 22:2: "The kingdom of heaven is like a king who prepared a wedding banquet for his son." From this verse spring the other details of the parable. The mistreated messengers, the king's anger, the guests gathered in the wedding hall, the man without the wedding garment—these result from the fact that the king prepared a banquet for his son. Or, let us rather say, God the Father has prepared a celebration for His Son, Jesus.

What is more joyous than a wedding banquet? Those occasions give workers a chance to savor their labor in the vineyard. That's why Scripture so often uses the picture of the wedding banquet. (Remember, we understand pictures more quickly than words!) For example, Isaiah 62:5: "As a young man marries a maiden, so will your sons marry you; as a bridegroom rejoices over his bride, so will your God rejoice over you." Or, Revelation 19:7: "Let us rejoice and be glad and give Him glory! For the wedding of the Lamb has come, and His bride has made herself ready." And verse 9 of the same chapter: "Blessed are those who are invited to the wedding supper of the Lamb!" So Jesus uses this festive picture of a wedding banquet to put the simple question: Are you with Me or against Me?

Some in the Savior's audience were wilfully against Him (22:3). "They refused to come." Some had their priorities mixed up (22:5). "They paid no attention and went off—one to his field, another to his business". Others were violently hostile. They (22:6) "seized his servants, mistreated them and killed them." It doesn't take much imagination to translate that into our modern idiom:

> "No, I don't want to have anything to do with the church."

> "Well, I'd like to, but I've got pressing things to do right now."

> Or, think about the persecution of Christians in lands where faith is not tolerated.

Each response to the invitation traces back to the speaker's response to Jesus Christ. Every rejection of faith talk, every postponement to a more-convenient time, and every hostile word or act come from people who don't want to come to the celebration that the King gives for His Son, Jesus Christ—the celebration right now and the future, eternal celebration of heaven.

Nonetheless (22:10), the Father will fill His banquet

hall. Compare this with John's description of heaven in Revelation 7:9. "After this I looked and there before me was a great multitude that no one could count, from every nation, tribe, people and language, standing before the throne and in front of the Lamb." This great multitude does not include those who have rejected the invitation. No, only those are chosen who are splendidly dressed, their robes washed in the blood of the Lamb (Revelation 7:14), and (22:11–13) wearing the garment of faith. By human standards, the chosen multitude is a ragtag lot. Pulled from the "street corners" (22:9–10), they appear to us "both good and bad." Yet it is not outward appearance, but penitent faith that accounts for their presence at the wedding banquet of the Son. They—we!—are there because of Jesus Christ.

3 What Do You Think about the Christ?

It's not always easy to pull a conversation around to talk about Jesus Christ. People far more readily debate the church's stand on abortion or the ordination of women. People far more gladly argue about infant Baptism or speaking in tongues. People willingly admit, "I believe in God but don't really want to talk about who that God is, what His Law demands, and what His Son has done." Faith talk, though, means little or nothing if it does not center on Jesus Christ.

A persistent refusal to come to Christ shortens the precious day of grace. Jesus' conversations in Matthew 21–22 get progressively shorter and more curt as He interacts with those who reject the Father's invitation.

First (22:15–17), the Pharisees and the Herodians try to trap Him by talking politics: "Tell us then, what is Your opinion? Is it right to pay taxes to Caesar or not?" Jesus does not directly answer the question but skillfully terminates the conversation. Next (22:23–33), come the Sadducees. Their denial of the resurrection prompted the tricky theological question in verse 28: "Whose wife will she be of the seven, since all of them were married to her?" Jesus' curt answer does not seem designed to win friends and influence people (22:29): "You are in error because you do not know the Scriptures or the power of God." He then goes on to explain that God instituted marriage for this world, not for heaven. That answer did win some friends and influence some people (22:33): "When the crowds heard this, they were astonished at His teaching." Finally (22:34–40), the Pharisees return. After cutting through their theological games with a simple "Love God and love your neighbor," Jesus takes the offensive in verses 41–46. Quoting Psalm 110:1, He asks how King David's Son can also be King David's Lord. Can a human descendant also be a divine ruler? Yes! And though it angers the Pharisees, the human and divine Lord David described is Jesus Himself. It all boils down to this (22:42): "What do you think about the Christ?"

Conclusion

That was the key question, really the only question, then and now. "What do you think about the Christ?" That is an urgent question. By and large, the Pharisees and Sadducees were confirmed in their opposition to Jesus. Their hearts were hardened. So Jesus does not practice a Dale Carnegie course with them. Proverbs 26:4 advises, "Do not answer a fool according to his folly." Jesus had no time for idle chatter that was not centered on His work as Messiah.

What about our words of witness? As we talk about Jesus with others do we merely exercise our minds, trying to impress others with our intelligence or argue them into seeing our way as the right way? Talk about the faith matters too much for that. It is serious. Urgent. Pressing. This is the day of grace. We must extend the invitation to penitent faith in Christ while it is still day. Peter writes (1 Peter 3:15): "Always be prepared to give an answer to everyone who asks you to give the reason for the hope that you have" So, yes. We do talk about "religion"—we talk about Jesus Christ and faith in Him. And we pray in confidence that our Lord will use our words of witness to create saving faith and fruitful lives in those who hear our words.

Concluding Activities

Distribute study leaflet 6 and encourage participants to read the articles "The Greatest Commandment?" and "What Is God Like?" on pages 4–6 of the enrichment magazine.

Lecture Leaders Session 6 — Matthew Part 2

Jesus Condemns His Unrepentant Opponents

Matthew 23

Preparing for the Session

Central Focus

Appearances are deceiving. Without God's Word, we are not only deceived but are led into the woes of despair and the condemnation of hell. However, in God's Word we have an infallible basis for faith and life.

Objectives

That the participant, as a child of God and with the Holy Spirit's help, will be led to

1. appreciate as never before that "The LORD does not look at the things man looks at. Man looks at the outward appearance, but the LORD looks at the heart" (1 Samuel 16:7);
2. depend upon God and His revealed Word;
3. let words of woe and condemnation drive him or her to the Savior.

Note for small-group leaders: Lesson notes and other materials you will need begin on page 79.

For the Lecture Leader

Bible passages are multifaceted diamonds. Viewed in different ways, they reveal fascinating truths. The greatest truth is God's salvation for us in Jesus Christ. His righteousness, not our own, brings us into the Kingdom. The Bible also teaches us what life in this world is really like. It teaches how human self-righteousness collides with the righteousness of Christ revealed in the Word. This week's lecture requires you to look at Matthew 23 in several ways, some of which may be totally new to you. You need to hear Jesus' woes upon the Pharisees and the teachers of the law and to understand why He condemns them. You also need to look at the chapter and see that the Pharisees and teachers of the law really did appear righteous to many of their contemporaries. Finally, you need to search the chapter to discover how we can have certainty even though we live in a world of confusing religious opinion. Give yourself ample time for study. This is a fascinating chapter!

Blessed Lord, since You have caused all Holy Scriptures to be written for our learning, grant that we may so hear them, read, mark, learn and take them to heart that by patience and comfort of Your holy Word we may embrace and ever hold fast the blessed hope of everlasting life; through Jesus Christ, Your Son, our Lord, who lives and reigns with You and the Holy Spirit, one God, now and forever. Amen.

The Collect for the Word, *Lutheran Worship*, p. 156.

Session Plan

Worship

Begin the session with the hymn and prayer printed in the study leaflet. Note that the accompaniment for the hymn can be found on the music CD that accompanies this course. If you plan to use it, find it on the disk and cue it up for easy use.

Devotion

Matthew has steeped his Gospel in the Old Testament. He assumes his readers know the Hebrew Scriptures. Nowhere is this more apparent than in the account of Jesus triumphal entry into Jerusalem. As we saw last time, Matthew quotes Psalm 118 again and again as he describes the first Palm Sunday. This promontory, or high point, provides a place on which to stand as we look back on the chapters of Matthew we've read so far and as we look forward to the accounts of the passion and resurrection that lie ahead.

As Jesus rode into Jerusalem on a borrowed donkey, He no doubt looked both back and ahead. He saw Calvary's cross; He saw the "nations" (Psalm 118:10–12) that would surround Him and attempt to destroy Him. He anticipated Satan's violence (118:12). Still, on He rode—to become our strength, our song, our salvation (118:14). He has become the "gate of the LORD" (118:20) through which we—righteous in His blood—may enter!

Hosanna means "save now" and comes from Psalm 118:25. Jesus answered that prayer the crowd prayed on Palm Sunday—but not in the way they had imagined. What aspects of Christ's salvation surprise you?

Lecture Presentation

This lecture also appears on the CD-ROM that accompanies this course. Also look at the PDFFILES directory on the CD-ROM for overhead transparency graphics for the course.

Introduction: "I Hope So-and-so Heard That Sermon!"

"I hope so-and-so heard that sermon!" Time now for true confessions: We've all had that thought at some time or other when the pastor thundered God's Law against sin. In a way, the thought isn't totally wrong. In fact, "I hope so-and-so heard that sermon" is a great way to get into chapter 23.

1 Woe!

Display visual 6A from the CD-ROM.

The Pharisees and the teachers of the law deserved the stinging words that Jesus unloaded in this chapter. Take a look at how He lets them have it. Verse 13: "Woe to you, teachers of the law and Pharisees, you hypocrites!" The exact same words are repeated in verses 15, 23, 25, 27, and 29. The "woe" in verse 16 is different but just as stinging: "Woe to you, blind guides!" This is followed by "You blind fools" in verse 17, "you blind guides" in verse 24, and "blind Pharisee" in verse 26. The name-calling climaxes in verse 33: "You snakes! You brood of vipers!" When we remember that Satan took on the form of a snake in Eden, we see just how powerful our Lord intends His accusation to be!

Jesus goes on in each case to give reasons for these woes. There is substance behind the names He hurls at the Pharisees and teachers of the law:

23:3—"They do not practice what they preach."

23:5—"Everything they do is done for men to see."

23:8–12—They exalt themselves.

23:13—They keep people out of the Kingdom.

23:15—They pursue mission prospects whom they train for hell.

23:16–22—They play word games with oaths.

23:23–24—They pay for true religion instead of practicing it.

23:25–26—Their love of ritual is simply a cloak that covers their greed and self-indulgence.

23:27–28—Their righteousness is an impressive facade that conceals hypocrisy and wickedness.

23:29–36—Their family tree is full of those who persecuted and murdered the prophets.

23:37–39—Jesus had wanted to gather Israel like a hen gathers her chicks, but their stubborn opposition will bring them divine retribution instead.

Oh, how Jesus' speech must have been animated! How His eyes must have blazed as He told those so-and-sos where they would go!

At this point most of us are probably ready to jump in and say, "Jesus, it's high time You let them have it!" We've been fed up with the evil antics of the Pharisees and teachers of the law for 22 chapters now. Like us today, probably some people in the Lord's first audience applauded Jesus' stinging attack. The people who followed current events in that day knew that Jesus had been at odds with the Pharisees and teachers of the law for some time. Many of the sincere common people felt oppressed by the tradition these spiritual leaders had laid on them (see Matthew 11:28–30). Other people, those who rankled under any kind of authority, were ready to rebel against the religious leadership simply because of the way these leaders had cooperated with

Rome. No doubt, plenty of people thought, I hope they're hearing every word of this.

2 Righteous Appearances

Jesus' words, however, confused many in the crowds. Whether they actually heard the Lord's sermon with their own ears or heard secondhand reports about it, many people must have felt perplexed or even upset by Jesus' vehement attack. The Pharisees and teachers of the law did have a fine outward appearance. Jesus Himself said (23:28): "On the outside you appear to people as righteous." People in general did not despise these leaders. They admired them! The reason many of us look in scorn at the Pharisees and teachers of the law is that our opinions have been shaped by the words of Jesus, the words of the omniscient Son of God whose eyes pierced through the appearance of piety to see the sin that lurked deep within the hearts. Jesus can do that. The rest of us, however, fallible as we are, usually find ourselves impressed by what we see. And outwardly the Pharisees and teachers of the law did look good.

Display visual 6B from the CD-ROM.

Let me take you now through parts of chapter 23 and show how the Pharisees and teachers of the law were treated by their contemporaries. Verse 2 says, "The teachers of the law and the Pharisees sit in Moses' seat." The words *Moses' seat* may refer to a special chair reserved for the president of the Sanhedrin or, in a more general sense, to the authority to teach among God's people. Now, ask yourself a commonsense question. Would the people have given such a responsible position to the Pharisees and teachers of the law? Would they have tolerated anyone holding this position of honor who was considered unworthy of such an office? Of course not.

Let's take another example. Verses 6–7 say, "They love the place of honor at banquets and the most important seats in the synagogues; they love to be greeted in the marketplaces and to have men call them 'Rabbi.'" Would the people have given the Pharisees and teachers of the law the places of honor or greeted them respectfully in public if they despised these leaders? I doubt that the Pharisees pushed and shoved like little children trying to be first in line at the drinking fountain. The people accorded the Pharisees places of honor and titles of respect quite likely because they truly did honor and respect them.

Another example. The phrase *greatest among you* in verse 11 implies that the devotees of the Pharisees and the teachers of the law debated the merits of their rabbis (e.g., "My rabbi is smarter than your rabbi!"). The people sought out their wisdom—in matters of speech, for instance. These leaders gave their opinions on the kinds of oaths that could and could not properly be made. In verse 18 Jesus says, "You also say, 'If anyone swears by the altar, it means nothing; but if anyone swears by the gift on it, he is bound by his oath.'" A modern parallel might be: "I know I shouldn't say hell, but is heck okay?" Jesus had no use for this kind of hairsplitting, coming as it did from unbelieving hearts. But, here's the present point. Students *did* seek out the learned opinions of the teachers of the law and the Pharisees on such religious questions. They *were* held in some esteem.

A final example. Verse 23 says, "You give a tenth of your spices—mint, dill and cummin. But you have neglected the more important matters of the law—justice, mercy and faithfulness. You should have practiced the latter, without neglecting the former." The tithing of garden spices like mint, dill, and cummin seems to go above and beyond the original tithing God commands in Leviticus 27:30 and Deuteronomy 14:22–29. The Pharisees left no stone unturned in their efforts to obey the letter of the Law. Still (23:23) when Jesus says that they should have practiced justice, mercy, and faithfulness, He cues us in to the truth: Their contributions had a fine outward appearance while their hearts remained self-focused and arrogant. Jesus piles on the Law, telling them God demands both strict observance of the rules outwardly *and* devotion in the heart. Here our Lord does not imply the Pharisees can earn favor with God by keeping the Law. Instead, He uses the severity of the Law to demonstrate the fact they cannot keep it. He wants them to despair of their own goodness and throw themselves on the mercy He freely provides the penitent sinners of every time and place. But they refuse that mercy.

3   1 Samuel 16:7

Display visual 6C from the CD-ROM.

This leads us to verses 27–28. "Woe to you, teachers of the law and Pharisees, you hypocrites! You are like whitewashed tombs, which look beautiful on the outside but on the inside are full of dead men's bones and everything unclean. In the same way, on the outside you appear to people as righteous but on the inside you are full of hypocrisy and wickedness."

The only reason we can applaud Jesus' attack on the Pharisees and teachers of the law is because Jesus, the all-knowing Son of God, stripped away their pious facade, laid bare their hypocrisy, and revealed it all to us in His inspired Word. Without His omniscience and revelation in Scripture, we would not know that the Pharisees and teachers of the law were hell-bound hypocrites, any more than we today can look into the heart of another person and pass judgment. 1 Samuel 16:7: "The LORD does not look at the things man looks at. Man looks at the outward appearance, but the LORD looks at the heart."

All of this should make us think twice as we form opinions about others—and about ourselves too! When we imagine that we can know someone's heart by observing their outward conduct, we are judging the unseen things of the spirit by external, visible evidence.

Suppose another person simply exudes Christianity. Always in church, always in Bible study, always talking about the Lord, always doing works in His name. Can we know a heart by such outward conduct? No! Jesus said, "Many will say to Me on that day, 'Lord, Lord, did we not prophesy in Your name, and in Your name drive out demons and perform many miracles?' Then I will tell them plainly, 'I never knew you. Away from Me, you evildoers!' " (7:22–23).

This is why Jesus so vehemently condemned the Pharisees and teachers of the law. They looked so good! But they were evil and unrepentant (23:28). "You appear to people as righteous but on the inside you are full of hypocrisy and wickedness."

(*Note: If someone asks about times Christians can and must judge, refer them to the article that discusses these concepts in the enrichment magazine for Matthew, Part 1.*)

4   The Word—Not Appearances

Appearances are deceiving. Whenever we venture past tentative opinions, we make the same mistake as the Pharisees who did everything (23:5) "for men to see." When we judge by appearances, we're heading for eventual despair. Not only are we wrongly judging others, we are—and this is important—also directing ourselves away from the divine Word and toward our own fallible observations and reason. Often we are tempted to do that; often we succumb. God's Word calls us back to the true path of discipleship: faith, not sight. Dr. Martin Luther said:

> *What a precious thing it is to have the Word of God on our side in everything we do! For such a person is safe, however much he may be tried. But without the Word a man of necessity finally falls into despair, for he lacks divine assurance for what he is called upon to do. He is borne onward merely by the egotism of his heart. This is why Psalm 119:21 praises the Word of God so highly and says: "Thou hast rebuked the proud that are cursed, which do err from Thy commandments," that is, prosperity will (in the end) not be theirs outside the Word of God, because "every plant which My heavenly Father hath not planted shall be rooted up" (Matthew 15:13), said Jesus.*

Ewald M. Plass, *What Luther Says* (St. Louis: Concordia, 1959).

So, what to do? Set our eyes on the Word! Turn our attention away from outward appearances and become more and more occupied with God's Word. Only God searches the heart, and only God's Word is the basis for belief. Hebrews 4:12–13: "For the word of God is living and active. Sharper than any double-edged sword, it penetrates even to dividing soul and spirit, joints and marrow; it judges the thoughts and attitudes of the heart. Nothing in all creation is hidden from God's sight. Everything is uncovered and laid bare before the eyes of Him to whom we must give account."

"You can't judge a book by its cover." Nor can you judge human beings by their external appearance. The cover of the Bible may not be inviting, but its contents are riveting, fascinating, for the Bible is the only reliable source of truth in our confusing world.

The Pharisees and the teachers of the law would not hear God's prophetic word. Satisfied with their own show of righteousness, they repeatedly rejected the Word of God sent through the prophets. Finally, they crucified the Word incarnate, Jesus Christ. We saw that in last week's lesson. In the parable of the tenants (21:33–46), the servants of the landowner were abused and his son was killed. In the parable of the wedding banquet (22:1–14), the king's repeated invitations to a joyous feast were consciously ignored.

So now in Matthew 23 Jesus lets the Pharisees and teachers of the law have it. He rebukes their fascination with outward appearances and their failure to hear the Word. His rebuke climaxes in verses 29–39:

> 23:31—"You are the descendants of those who murdered the prophets."
>
> 23:34—"I am sending you prophets and wise men and teachers. Some of them you will kill and crucify; others you will flog in your synagogues and pursue from town to town."
>
> 23:38–39—"Your house is left to you desolate. For I tell you, you will not see Me again until you say, 'Blessed is He who comes in the name of the Lord'."

Dr. Martin Luther wrote:

> *Our Lord God is a Preacher who delivers His sermon in such a way that all the world hears it and yet no one but the godly understand it. Just so these high priests, the scribes, and Herod have the prophet [Micah] on their lips and in their ears but understand as much of him as a cow does.*

Plass, *What Luther Says.*

Conclusion: Embracing Love

We've heard the woes, and we've heard the condemnations. We've seen how these things apply to our own lives. We realize that many times in the past we *knew* but did not *do* what our Lord wanted. We've put on a good show of piety for all to see, but on the inside—deep down where it counts—our hearts have remained as numb and hollow as the hearts of the Pharisees. God's Law has convicted us of hypocrisy.

Display visual 6D from the CD-ROM.

That's where our Lord—in love—begins with us. He proclaims Law for the sake of the Gospel. By the threats of that Law we see our need for our Savior. We've stopped hoping someone else heard the sermon and thank God *we* have. You see (23:37), Jesus wants to gather us, His brothers and sisters, to Himself just as a hen gathers her chicks under her wings to hide them, to protect them from the circling predator or from the fire licking around the foundation of the chicken house. Satan circles. Death and God's judgment threaten to destroy us, but in Jesus, under His wings, in the shadow of His cross, we find refuge. Rest in His total pardon of all your sins today. Sleep in the peace of that pardon tonight. Ask the Holy Spirit to change your outward religion into an ever deepening relationship with your heavenly Father.

Concluding Activities

Distribute study leaflet 7 and encourage participants to include in their preparation for next week "Keep Watch!" and "Our Mission to the Least of These" on pages 27–31 of the enrichment magazine.

Notes

Jesus Prepares His Disciples for the End Times

Matthew 24–25

Preparing for the Session

Central Focus

In the hymn "God of Grace and God of Glory," Harry Emerson Fosdick wrote words terribly true of our society: *Rich in things and poor in soul.* Jesus' prophecies about the end of the world teach us to be critical of contemporary society and help us ready our souls for His return.

Objectives

That the participant, as a child of God and with the help of the Holy Spirit, will be led to

1. value more highly the things of the soul;
2. develop a more biblical attitude toward time;
3. become more critically aware of our society;
4. lose self in service to Christ.

Note for small-group leaders: Lesson notes and other materials you will need begin on page 82.

For the Lecture Leader

As you read these chapters in the Bible, keep one fact in mind. Here our Lord prophesies both the destruction of Jerusalem (which occurred in A.D. 70) and the end of the world (which will occur in …). These two prophecies are so intimately entwined that they often cannot be separated to ease our human interpretation. Certain verses, however, that first appear difficult to explain become easier when the presence of two prophecies is remembered. Consider this possible interpretation:

24:4–14 describe the world at the end of time;

24:15–22 deal with the invasion of Jerusalem and its destruction by the Roman general Titus in A.D. 70;

24:23–31 comment on Christ's return in glory to judge the living and the dead.

The lecture attempts to say much more than "We don't know when Jesus will return; therefore we should always be ready." While that is very, very true, we need to learn *how* to be ready. The lecture attempts to pull some suggestions out of the biblical text that will help us Christians be faithful and wise servants. Fosdick observed that our society is "Rich in things and poor in soul." We join him in praying, "Grant us wisdom, grant us courage lest we miss Your kingdom's goal, lest we miss Your kingdom's goal."

Session Plan

Worship

If possible, begin the session by darkening the room (leaving exits lighted). Ask one of the participants (plan ahead of time) to read the prayer. Then bring the lights up just enough so participants can see to sing the hymn printed in the study leaflet. Or simply play two or three stanzas of the hymn and invite participants to think about Christ's return as they listen. The accompaniment for the hymn can be found on the music CD that accompanies this course. If you plan to use it, find it on the disk and cue it up for easy use.

Devotion

The ability to play the piano. The gift of teaching. Athletic prowess. All these come from God. They testify to His love for us. But they are not what Jesus had in mind when He told the parable recorded in Matthew 25:14–30. The word *talent* used in the text comes to us from the world of ancient financial customs and first referred to a specific amount of silver by weight. In today's money markets, a talent would be valued at more than $1,000.

As our Lord imported this term into His parable, He used it to represent what we might call "a golden opportunity." Each servant in our Lord's story had a chance to serve the king. Not all had the same opportunities. All produced different returns on their investments. But all who were faithful were also fruitful.

You may at times feel quite useless in Christ's kingdom. But you can intercede for Christ's kingdom! You may work at a thankless, low-paying job. But you can watch for opportunities to show love and to speak about the love of Jesus! You may head up a large corporation or may pastor a small church. But even in your busyness, you can look for ways to do what Jesus would do, to say what Jesus would say if He sat in your chair.

The unfaithful servant of 25:24–25 didn't know the king at all. See how he describes him? When we know Jesus' self-sacrificing death for us, when we've seen His tender compassion and forgiveness, His love changes us! By His grace, then, we can be faithful *and* fruitful!

Lecture Presentation

This lecture also appears on the CD-ROM that accompanies this course. Also look at the PDFFILES directory on the CD-ROM for overhead transparency graphics for the course.

Introduction: Perfect Body, Perfect Soul

Can you picture the perfect body? You probably can. One of the most common images today is the perfect—or almost perfect—body. The people who make it onto the television screen are good-looking people. Commercials usually make their pitch with the help of a perfect body. Usually that body is doing nothing important, just arousing our appetites. You've probably noticed the proliferation of health clubs and their aggressive recruiting campaigns. Maybe you belong to a club like that. If you do, if you eat right and exercise, you are being a good steward, a good caretaker, of the body our Creator has given you. But in any case, I'm quite sure that you can picture the perfect body.

Now—can you picture the perfect soul? Think about that. Can you picture the perfect soul? *(pause)* I would guess that no image jumped into your mind. Of course, the soul is not a material object. The soul transcends purely physical life, but it's hard to imagine ourselves without our body. The perfect soul is not a preoccupation of too many people in our society; although more people think about such things today than they did a few decades or so ago. Even though our society thinks of itself as "more spiritual" now, the perfect soul is still not something people, in general, pursue.

It is *our* pursuit, as Christ's people, however. Following Christ does not require the perfect body, but it will require your soul. Our quest to know Christ more and more through faith means that we are pursuing an ever more perfect soul. In theological words, we are striving after greater sanctification (holiness or godliness). St. Paul wrote, "Physical training is of some value, but godliness has value for all things, holding promise for both the present life and the life to come" (1 Timothy 4:8). So, in today's review of Matthew 24–25 let me describe to you a more perfect soul.

1 Society's Perfect Carcass

The more perfect soul is developed against the background of the glorious Christ coming on the clouds of heaven to judge the living and the dead. This soul has developed a keen sensitivity to the eternal, even as it goes about mundane, daily affairs. The pagan Romans used to say, *memento mori*, remember death. Each day we remember death with the anticipation of seeing Christ. 1 Peter 1:8–9: "Though you have not seen Him, you love Him; and even though you do not see Him now, you believe in Him and are filled with an inexpressible and glorious joy, for you are receiving the goal of your faith, the salvation of your souls." This anticipation permeates the thoughts of the mind; it fills the heart with joy; it gives the soul an inexhaustible supply of hope. Christ is going to come back visibly. He's going to come back for you and me!

Display visual 7A from the CD-ROM.

Our question is, "When?" The disciples asked this question too (24:3): "When will this happen, and what will be the sign of Your coming and of the end of the age?" In these words, the disciples really asked two questions: "When will Jerusalem be destroyed?" and "When will

You return for Judgment Day?" Jesus answers both questions at the same time, a fact which helps explain some otherwise difficult verses. Here's one possible way to interpret each part of our Lord's answer:

Verses 4–14 describe the world at the end of time.

Verses 15–22 deal with the destruction of Jerusalem in A.D. 70 when the Roman general Titus laid seige to the city and razed it.

Verses 23–31 tell about our Lord's return to earth as Judge and King on the Last Day.

Jesus' answer to His disciples' questions concerning the end of the world and Jerusalem's destruction contains many signs, not just the one sign that the disciples had requested:

24:6—Wars and rumors of war

24:7—Famines and earthquakes

24:9—Hatred and persecution of true Christians

24:10—Apostasy, that is, "many will turn away from the faith"

24:10—A spiteful society where people—even supposed Christians—"will betray and hate each other"

24:15—The abomination that causes desolation

24:24—Great signs and miracles

24:5, 23–24, 26—Persuasive and deceptive Christs

24:29—Cosmic signs

Finally, our Lord promises (24:14): "This gospel of the kingdom will be preached in the whole world as a testimony to all nations, and then the end will come."

Some of these signs have appeared from the first century onward—wars and famines, for example. Certainly Christians have faced persecution since the beginning. Even so, more Christians were martyred in the 20th century then in all 19 prior centuries combined! Many have turned from the faith. And more and more people groups on earth have had the chance to hear and believe the Gospel. Few tribes live in such remote places that they have had no access to Christian teaching.

But what is the (24:15) "abomination that causes desolation"? Daniel foretold this and his words were fulfilled in 168 B.C. as Antiochus Epiphanes erected an altar to Zeus in the temple. Some see a further fulfillment when the soldiers of Titus surrounded Jerusalem. In fact, as Titus arrived with his armies, some Christian fled to the hills as the Lord had urged in 24:16–20 and found refuge in Pella, in the Transjordan Mountains.

Even though some of Jesus' prophecies have already been fulfilled, the most ominous ones lay still in the future. With such terrible signs of the impending end, doesn't it strike you as very strange that our society is preoccupied with building the perfect physical body? People's ignorance of spiritual matters and their preoccupation with things (materialism) does, in fact, render our society vulnerable to damning religious counterfeits, to (24:24) "false Christs and false prophets." As Jesus says (24:28): "Wherever there is a carcass, there the vultures will gather." The coming of our Lord will be as obvious as the location of a carcass newly discovered by vultures. Yet, still, some will miss the signs.

2 Numbering Our Days

Display visual 7B from the CD-ROM.

We're in Bible study to develop with the Spirit's grace an ever more sanctified soul. These signs of the end times teach us that a soul moving toward perfection is not disengaged from society. Quite to the contrary, the soul is *in* the body and you, Christian, body and soul, are *in* the world—though not "of the world." Being in the world demands a critical knowledge of what's going on about us. A soul engaged with the world is not content simply to read the newspapers and watch the evening news, though we do indeed do that, in part to inform ourselves as good citizens and in part to gather topics for our daily prayers. Still, knowing what's going on in this world requires us to bring together sociology, law, medicine, and all the other disciplines of learning our wise Creator made available to us. We study them under the inspired and guiding light of God's Word. Of course, none of us can know all the secular disciplines. Each, however, can know a little, and together we Christians can have that critical perspective that tests the spirits.

St. John says (1 John 4:1): "Dear friends, do not believe every spirit, but test the spirits to see whether they are from God, because many false prophets have gone out into the world." Our society is going to run faster and faster, scattering hither and yon whenever the media reports new visions; new apparitions, ghosts, or miracles; new philosophies; new religions; new angels; new anythings. Just as Jesus said, we will hear (24:23): "Look, here is the Christ!" or "There he is!" Our Lord urges us not to believe it! The ever more perfect soul is a skeptic, an "unbeliever" of sorts, if you will. Our minds stay occupied with words and teachings from Scripture and studied reflection about our contemporary society.

The soul pursuing perfection is always ready for the return of the Son of Man. We see all around us the signs that tell us He is coming. Paul says (Romans 13:11): "Salvation is nearer now than when we first believed." But the exact date and time are unknown (24:36). "No one knows about that day or hour, not even the angels in heaven, nor the Son, but only the Father." Does it seem strange to you that Jesus doesn't know? How can we explain this "lapse"? Our Lord spoke these words during His earthly state of humiliation. During that time He voluntarily restricted the use of His divine knowledge. When He gave us verse 36 He did not use His divine omniscience. Perhaps He did that to make the lesson more emphatic for you and me (24:44). "You also must be ready, because the Son of Man will come at an hour when you do not expect Him."

Therefore, the ever more perfect soul is a good steward of time. Jesus asked (24:45): "Who then is the faithful and wise servant?" To endure the troubles of our earth's last days, Jesus says we need to be both *faithful* and *wise*. We need wisdom to understand the true nature of time. Our society has debased time to the point it amounts to nothing more than a measuring stick used to prioritize one's personal goals. Time, however, is not incidental to our pursuits. We live in time. God has put us here to do his will. Time belongs to God, not to us. The faithful and wise servant knows that we borrow each day; it comes to us as a gift of God to be used for doing His work in the world. Sooner or later, on Judgment Day or at the time of your death, God will reclaim time.

To prepare for that unknown day and hour, the ever more perfect soul faithfully surrenders time each day to God. Significant time spent in devotion, worship, Bible study, and service show that we realize all time belongs to God. How different is our contemporary society! "I don't have time," they say. "Do you have a minute?" they ask. Most common expressions about time reveal the assumption that time is ours, that it belongs to us. This insidious view of time shows up in Christian hearts whenever we think or say, "I don't have time for devotions" or "I don't have time for weekly worship." God help us live as faithful servants, and also wise servants! With Moses we pray (Psalm 90:12): "Teach us to number our days aright, that we may gain a heart of wisdom."

3 Useful Servants

The ever more perfect soul who practices the daily surrender of time to God is a soul conversant with God and ready for His final summons. Perhaps some of you who grew up in a church family had a mother who said every Saturday night, "There's church tomorrow. Time for your bath." So the parable of the virgins teaches us that Christ the bridegroom is coming, and we must be practiced and ready for His advent. In this parable the Scriptures offer another critical insight into the abuse of time by our society, that well-developed carcass that is prey to false prophets and false Christs. Did you notice that the foolish virgins were looking forward to the marriage feast? They assumed that heaven would be theirs. Yet their eternal destiny was not so important that they would devote to it "their" time. How many people today identify themselves as Christians and assume that heaven is their due? These people, like the foolish virgins, are unpracticed in meeting God. They don't know the daily conversations with God that spring from repentant faith in the Savior. Since they are unpracticed now in the saving faith, they will be unprepared to meet the bridegroom when He comes. The soul sanctified more and more by the Holy Spirit rehearses daily for the final eternal meeting. Though "the bridegroom [be] a long time in coming" (25:5), the ever more perfect soul acknowledges Him as the ever present Lord of grace who gives His servants the mercy and faith we do not deserve and have not earned.

Such a soul is useful to God. If you owned a business (maybe you do), how would you feel about an employee who did little or nothing to improve your company? Likewise, the man in the parable of the talents was most upset with the servant who said (25:25): "I was afraid and went out and hid your talent in the ground. See, here is what belongs to you." Does God need us to protect what is already His own? Of course not. God can take care of His own. We His servants are to advance His cause in our society with our faithful efforts. It is not for us to decide whether we will or will not do the work of the Lord. Since we confess Him as our Lord and Savior, our decision is *how* to do His work most effectively.

Did you wonder what that worthless servant did after he dug a hole in the ground and hid his master's money? He obviously went about his own business or pleasure, not the master's. He did what pleased him, not his lord. By that sloth he claimed dominion over his rightful master.

The truth here is obvious. Our sloth in doing the work of the Lord amounts to a denial that God in Christ is our rightful Lord. If our business or our pleasure guides our thoughts and activities, we are in effect refusing to submit to our Lord, our rightful Master.

4 No Records Kept

Now the final quality of ever more perfect souls. They are forgetful. Surprising? Maybe some of you belong to a health club. The people who lift weights keep a record of how much they lift and how many repetitions they've done. Sometimes they just remember it; other times, they write it all down. That's part of building the perfect body. How different the perfect soul! It hardly remembers from day to day the good things done for the Lord. Look at 25:37–39: "Lord, when did we see You hungry and feed You, or thirsty and give You something to drink? When did we see You a stranger and invite You in, or needing clothes and clothe You? When did we see You sick or in prison and go to visit You?" Are you one of these people? They don't keep track of what they have done, because they are not promoting their own cause. They're not interested in hanging medals on a perfect soul. They reject a righteousness based on their own works. The return of Christ and the work of His kingdom preoccupy them. They think and plan and consider how to introduce the Savior to more and more people! Who cares about keeping selfish records and collecting medals? We do everything we do all for Him.

Conclusion: Perfect Soul or Perfect Body?

Perfect soul or perfect body? For which have you been laboring? Our society's preoccupation with itself has turned it into a carcass waiting for false prophets and false Christs to prey on it. How sad it will be when so many of our contemporaries find out too late that they should have exercised their soul. Richard Baxter, the 17th-century author of *The Saints' Everlasting Rest*, puts these words on the lips of a person who realized too late the importance of caring for the soul:

> *How many weeks, and months, and years did I lose, which if I had improved, I might now have been happy! Wretch that I was! Could I find no time to study the work, for which I had all my time? no time, among all my labors, to labor for eternity? Had I time to eat, and drink, and sleep, and none to save my soul? Had I time for mirth and vain discourse, and none for prayer? Could I take time to secure the world, and none to try my title to heaven? O precious time! I had once enough, and now I must have no more. I had once so much, I knew not what to do with it; and now it is gone, and cannot be recalled. O that I had but one of those years to live over again! how speedily would I repent! how earnestly would I pray! how diligently would I hear! how closely would I examine my state! how strictly would I live!*

Richard Baxter, *The Saints' Everlasting Rest* (London: The Epworth Press, 1962).

Perfect body or perfect soul?

What do you choose to pursue?

Concluding Activities

Distribute study leaflet 8 and encourage participants to read "Real Presence, Real Comfort" on pages 12–13 of the enrichment magazine.

Notes

Lecture Leaders Session 8 — Matthew Part 2

Jesus Redeems Disciples in the Crisis of the Cross

Matthew 26–27

Preparing for the Session

Central Focus

Judas, Peter, and Jesus. One didn't survive. One did, only by forgiving grace. And one died and rose to give us His Holy Spirit that we might know and love Him more and more. The study of these three can equip our faith to withstand our times of crisis.

Objectives

That the participant, as a child of God and with the Holy Spirit's help, will be led to

1. appreciate the real life crises of Judas, Peter, and Jesus;
2. make zealous use of the calm times in life, "before the days of trouble come" (Ecclesiastes 12:1);
3. make the death of Christ the constant occupation of a willing spirit, in prayer, in worship, in remembrance, and in confident hope.

Note for small-group leaders: Lesson notes and other materials you will need begin on page 86.

For the Lecture Leader

Approach this lecture with the *via negativa*, the negative way. This lecture cannot say all that could be said about our Savior's passion recorded in Matthew 26 and 27. It cannot present a full doctrinal presentation of all that Christ's death means for us sinners. Time will not allow us to treat in full depth the institution of the Lord's Supper, the significant use of Old Testament quotations by Matthew, the rending of the veil, the opening of the tombs, and many other things.

In fact, these chapters of Matthew's Gospel defy adequate treatment for, given the Spirit's divine economy of words, we stand in awe before an overwhelming truth: God's own Son dies for us sinners. If this lecture kindles awe and sparks a greater desire for prayer, Word, and Sacrament we can be thankful, eternally thankful.

This week's Scripture stands at the very heart of the mystery of God's love for us as He gives His one and only Son into death for us on the cross. As you meet with your group this week, make it a time of praise to Jesus for His sacrifice, a time of thanksgiving to the Father for His most wonderful gift of salvation. Let your group sense your own wonder and awe at God's love for us. Let your feelings about what God has done for you be evident; wear your heart on your sleeve in this week's session.

Session Plan

Worship

Sing the hymn printed in the study leaflet. Use the music CD for accompaniment as needed. Then darken the room and have someone read the prayer found in the study leaflet for this week. (You will have to recruit someone before the assembly to do this and furnish the reader with a small flashlight.)

Devotion

In no section of Scripture can we read a more powerful contrast between Jesus' divine nature and His human nature than in this week's readings from our Lord's Passion. Here we read the plain truth that Jesus is true man and also that He is true God. What a mystery!

At its heart, the Christian faith as a whole is a mystery. We can express it, but not explain it, not really. The sinless Son of God died a hideous death in our place. He took our punishment; now we can claim His righteousness. No finite human mind, much less a sin-damaged mind, can comprehend the *hows* of it.

The *whys*, though, are another story. When we juxtapose the mockery, the beatings, the pain, and the crucifixion of Matthew 26–27 with the words of John 3:16, the *why* of Calvary explodes in all its glory:

God so loved … that He gave His one and only Son.

The *so* in that verse deserves all the emphasis we can muster. Even then, it's not enough. Overwhelming love drove God the Son to the manger and from the manger to the cross.

O depth of love, to me revealing
The sea where my sins disappear!
In Christ my wounds find perfect healing,
There is no condemnation here;
For Jesus' blood through earth and skies
Forever "Mercy! Mercy!" cries.

Johann A. Rothe, 1688–1758, alt.

Lecture Presentation

This lecture also appears on the CD-ROM that accompanies this course. Also look at the PDFFILES directory on the CD-ROM for overhead transparency graphics for the course.

Introduction: A Solemn Experience

Holy Week. Jesus dies. What can you say about it? What insight can we add in some feeble lecture? If you have ever visited the Vietnam Memorial in Washington, D.C., you sensed the subdued mood of the visitors. Few speak in the shadow of that wall. It is a solemn experience. For us, Holy Week and the death of Jesus set an even more solemn tone. God dies on a cross, nailed there by outwardly religious people, nailed there as a ransom for you and me. In this lecture we will look at Jesus, Peter, and Judas. Their experiences on that first Holy Week should sober us. One of the three did not survive. One did, only by forgiving grace. And one died and rose to give us His Holy Spirit so that we might know and love Him more and more.

Jesus, I will ponder now
On Your holy Passion;
With Your Spirit me endow
For such meditation.
Grant that I in love and faith
May the image cherish
Of Your suff'ring, pain, and death
That I may not perish.

Sigismund von Birken; tr. August Crull, alt.

1 Judas

Judas. The standard line about Judas is, "If he had only repented like Peter he would have been forgiven." That line is true and is probably sufficient at a Sunday school level of instruction, but it is too quick a dismissal for our in-depth Bible study. If you have ever suffered from depression or tried to encourage someone who is depressed, you know that even the most truthful words can seem ineffective. Even when the depressed person acknowledges that what you say is true, hope and joy do not immediately follow. Why did Judas despair to such an extent that he took his own life?

Or the more immediate question: Why did Judas betray Jesus? *(pause)* It probably wasn't for the money. Thirty pieces of silver was about three months' wages. Not bad money, but as treasurer for the Twelve (John 12:6), Judas could have done better by continuing his habit of embezzling over a long time frame.

Others have suggested that Judas wanted to force Jesus' hand. Remember that none of the disciples had understood the passion predictions. Judas may have assumed that Jesus' journey to Jerusalem marked the beginning of the long-awaited rebellion against Rome. Judas may have believed that Jesus was frittering away the momentum gained by His triumphal entry. Therefore, a "betrayal" would force Jesus into action. This explanation is plausible, but tentative. Scripture does not reveal the thoughts that led Judas to his terrible sin.

The Old Testament Book of Deuteronomy suggests a fascinating theological reason for the betrayal. Deuteronomy 13:1–5 describes false prophets and what to do with them. What if Judas had decided that Jesus was a false prophet? Listen to the text.

If a prophet, or one who foretells by dreams, appears among you and announces to you a miraculous sign or wonder, and if the sign or wonder of which he has spoken takes place, and he says, "Let us follow other gods" (gods you have not known) "and let us worship them," you must not listen to the words of that prophet or dreamer. The LORD your God is testing you to find out whether you love Him with all your heart and with all your soul. It is the LORD your God you must follow, and Him you must revere. Keep His commands and obey Him; serve Him and hold fast to Him. That prophet or dreamer must be put to death.

It is interesting to note that medieval Jewish commentators did identify Jesus with this text. If Judas had come to think of Jesus as a false prophet, then his betrayal was motivated by a sincere—but sadly misguided—religious zeal. This suggestion, although tentative, is intriguing because it revolves around the ultimate question for Judas and for us all (Matthew 22:41): "What do you think about the Christ?"

Whatever the scenario for the betrayal, Judas realized by early Friday that he had done wrong (27:3–4): "When Judas, who had betrayed Him, saw that Jesus was condemned, he was seized with remorse and returned the thirty silver coins to the chief priests and the elders. 'I have sinned,' he said, 'for I have betrayed innocent blood.'" Why did Judas not go beyond his remorse and look to Jesus for forgiveness? Hadn't Jesus taught him to pray "Forgive us our trespasses"? Why did Judas not fully repent? This is an important question. Why he betrayed Jesus makes for intriguing mental exercise, but why he did not seek forgiveness matters for us personally in all those times when we find ourselves tempted to lose hope in a gracious and forgiving God.

Display visual 8A from the CD-ROM.

Our answer must center in Christ. Judas did not see in Jesus the Christ of prophecy, nor did he perceive the depth of the Savior's love for sinners. He had squandered his time of grace and now could not withstand the crisis.

26:6–13—Judas had complained about the anointing at Bethany. Why didn't he emulate the woman's love for Jesus?

26:17–25—Judas was Jesus' guest for most of the Passover meal. Didn't that shared remembrance of God's deliverance stir greater affection for Jesus?

Didn't anything on Holy Thursday give Judas pause? We like to think we would have seen the train of shame and guilt coming and changed direction, but Judas misused the times of grace God gave him. Isaiah 55:6 warns: "Seek the LORD while He may be found; call on Him while He is near." Judas hadn't done that. Had he listened humbly to Jesus and searched the Old Testament Scriptures, he would have known Jesus to be the true and amazingly forgiving Christ, the Messiah. But, since Judas had not kept God's commands with all his heart and soul as Deuteronomy 13 required, he betrayed Jesus and lost hope in God's forgiving grace. Judas is a tragic example of Ecclesiastes 12:1: "Remember your Creator in the days of your youth, before the days of trouble come and the years approach when you will say, 'I find no pleasure in them.'"

But what about us? Today we enjoy God's day of grace. Today we have the written Scriptures. Today we can receive the Holy Supper. Today we have the chance to meet with other believers for prayer, for worship, for study, for mutual encouragement. May God the Holy Spirit give us His gift of repentance for the times when we've failed to make full use of His means of grace, and may He stir up within our hearts a deep yearning for the Word and Sacrament so that we can resist temptation in times of trial and darkness!

2 Peter

In Judas we see this truth: We need to learn to know God in Christ as deeply as we can during the peaceful times of life. We need to prepare by immersing ourselves in God's grace before the times of testing come. As we do this, we can learn from Peter's encouraging story. Yes, *encouraging*. Unlike Judas, Peter did not fall headlong into a hopeless outlook on life. Peter's sin deserved damnation every bit as much as Judas' betrayal did. Peter was beside himself because of his denial, somehow Peter's hope revived, and he continued in his discipleship. Peter's experiences in Holy Week provide a positive example for us. They show how faith can recover after a serious, depressing sin. They show us how to ready ourselves during the times of grace. "Therefore," says Psalm 32:6, "Let everyone who is godly pray to You while You may be found; surely when the mighty waters rise, they will not reach him." Matthew 26 suggests at least three characteristics of faith that helped Peter through his crisis—a God-given, willing spirit; prayer; and remembering. Let's look at these one by one.

Display visual 8B from the CD-ROM.

First, Peter led with his heart. In 26:41, Jesus analyzed Peter's sleep during the crucial time in Gethsemane: "The spirit is willing, but the body is weak." Peter's spirit was willing. He had told Jesus (26:33): "Even if all fall away on account of You, I never will." Peter was concerned about the betrayal (John 13:24): "Simon Peter motioned to this disciple [John] and said, 'Ask Him which one He means.'" John 21:17 tells us that after Holy Week had passed, Jesus asked Peter "Do you love Me?" Peter replied, "Lord, You know all things; You know that I love You." Yes, Peter's spirit was willing. The Holy Spirit had worked true faith in Peter's heart, just as He has in ours. Even so, we know our own weakness firsthand, just as Peter would soon know his, just as he would soon fall asleep in Gethsemane and fall into denial inside the high priest's courtyard. Even willing spirits falter. Think of the times you sin despite your best intentions.

So Jesus offers Peter—and us—a corrective (26:41): "Watch and pray so that you will not fall into temptation." Peter's prayer life wasn't perfect—Gethsemane provides one glaring example—but Peter had often had animated conversations with Jesus. For example, he was one of the disciples who took the initiative in asking (26:17): "Where do You want us to make preparations for You to eat the Passover?"

The night of the Passover, Jesus washed the disciples' feet (John 13:6–9): "He came to Simon Peter, who said to Him, 'Lord, are You going to wash my feet?' Jesus replied, 'You do not realize now what I am doing, but later you will understand.' 'No,' said Peter, 'You shall never wash my feet.' Jesus answered, 'Unless I wash you, you have no part with Me.' 'Then, Lord,' Simon Peter replied, 'not just my feet but my hands and my head as well!'"

Today we'd call that a lively prayer life! When Jesus predicted Peter's denial, Peter talked right back (26:35): "Even if I have to die with You, I will never disown You." That's the way it was with Peter. Think back to other stories we've studied. Peter asks Jesus to call him out to walk on water. Peter rejects Jesus' announcement about His coming suffering and death. Peter offers to erect shelters on the Mount of Transfiguration. Such lively conversations with the Savior helped Peter to grow in faith. That faith did not evaporate when Peter failed to watch and pray in Gethsemane.

Yes, Peter's faith faltered—seriously—but his hope did revive. Your prayer life, too, can ready you for the times when your willing spirit falters. This happens as you wrestle in prayer with your Lord over His Word. Just as Peter struggled to understand and to take to heart the words of the Savior, so also we, too, grow as by the grace of God we make His Word our own. When we limit our prayer lives only to asking for things, we also limit our spiritual growth. Bible study ought to be a dialogue in which we ask our Lord for deeper understanding. He will respond to our questions. He will deepen our faith. He will open up His mysteries to us as we read His Word and ask for insight and for His power to put it into practice in our lives.

We talk to God, and we also hear and ponder His words back to us. These words help us remember important truths that keep us from despair, even if we fall into gross and shameful sin. Throughout St. Matthew's Gospel, we have seen the Holy Spirit remind us of His Word from the Old Testament. How often haven't we read words like Matthew 26:56: "This has all taken place that the writings of the prophets might be fulfilled"? Remembering the Word of Jesus brought Peter to an almost immediate confession of his sin (26:74–75): "Immediately a rooster crowed. Then Peter remembered the word Jesus had spoken: 'Before the rooster crows, you will disown Me three times.'"

You and I do well, therefore, to remember the words of

Scripture. We ask children to memorize Scripture, but we adults need to commit more and more Bible passages to memory too. Often we treat the Holy Scripture like the Indianapolis 500, speeding across its pages so we can get on with life's tasks for the day. If we do that, then when times of despair come, we will lack the strength we need. In such times, we may not have it in us to sign up for an in-depth Bible study course, but we can have passages of hope committed to memory. "Memory," the ancients said, "is the guardian of treasures." For us, memory preserves precious words of the hope and forgiveness that belong to us in Jesus. If, by God's grace, you add memory of God's Word to daily and active meditation on God's Word, that Word will sustain you in the time of testing. In fact, had Peter used memory, prayer, and the power of the Spirit in the courtyard, he would not have denied his Savior! (Check Psalm 119:11.)

3 Jesus

And now, we turn to Jesus. What were the crises of Judas and Peter compared to those of Jesus in Holy Week? What are the crises of our lives compared to what He suffered? The words of the thief on the cross are true for us all (Luke 23:41): "We are punished justly, for we are getting what our deeds deserve. But this man has done nothing wrong." Judas had said the same (Matthew 27:4): "I have betrayed innocent blood." Pilate's wife, named Procula by tradition, said (27:19): "Don't have anything to do with that innocent man." Pilate knew Jesus was innocent (27:18): "It was out of envy that they had handed Jesus over to him." The centurion summarized (27:54): "Surely He was the Son of God." Remembering the sufferings of our innocent Savior, we find the greatest strength for our own times of despair.

The crises of Holy Week had always been out there, someplace off in the future for Jesus. The 12-year-old child in the temple, determined to be about His Father's business, had more recently (Luke 9:51) "resolutely set out for Jerusalem." Now the suffering drew nearer. Jesus told the disciples (26:18): "My appointed time is near." He readied Himself perfectly for the end. We learn much from Judas. We learn more from Peter. We learn the most about how to survive crises from Jesus Himself.

First, our Lord readied Himself by celebrating the Passover with His disciples. This remembrance of the Exodus was no empty ritual for Jesus. It provided a rich reminder of the salvation He had provided for ancient Israel. Now, Jesus was about to provide full salvation for all people. Not deliverance from earthly slavery in Egypt, but salvation from slavery of soul to sin and Satan, hell and death, lay at stake. Jesus wanted His disciples to remember forever the deliverance He would now provide, so He took some of the Passover bread and wine and invested in it a far deeper meaning than even the centuries-old Seder meal had held (26:26–28): "Take and eat; this is My body. … Drink from it, all of you. This is My blood of the covenant, which is poured out for many for the forgiveness of sins."

No need to debate those words. Would the Lord try to confuse His disciples as He spoke His last words to them the night before He died? Surely not! Jesus said just what He meant! The disciples received Christ's true body and true blood along with the bread and wine that night. These holy elements served as a focal point for worship as together Jesus and the disciples remembered God's salvation.

No, the disciples didn't understand the events that were about to overtake them. No, they didn't realize the full significance of the Sacrament Jesus held out to them. But they believed and they worshiped. Shouldn't we face our own crises in a spirit of worship? Word and Sacrament shared with fellow disciples is neither an empty ritual nor an optional social activity. In the Sacrament, God works in each of us and in all of us "for the forgiveness of sins." The disciples with whom we share this holy meal are imperfect. Some Judases may even defect. Some Peters deny their Lord in word and action. Still, week by week our Lord comes to us to impart forgiveness, hope, and the power of the Spirit to amend sinful lives. All this, in the Word and Sacrament.

Severe trials push us hard. The hours we spend in worship serve as only a prelude to a harsh week. Jesus readied Himself for the harsh events of Good Friday by adding solitude and prayer to His Passover observance and the institution of His Holy Supper. In solitude and prayer we commit to God our fears and needs. We ask for what we want and then experience the peace of turning our circumstances over to Him (26:39): "Not as I will, but as You will." Had Peter done this in Gethsemane instead of sleeping, probably he would not have denied Christ. Prepared by the time He had spent with His Father, Jesus was ready to say (26:45–46): "Look, the hour is near, and the Son of Man is betrayed into the hands of sinners. Rise, let us go!" How much time do you spend in solitude? in prayer?

Now Judas comes, Jesus is arrested, and the crisis is fully upon Him. Jesus shows Himself to be Christ-centered. He alone is the Christ. In the appearances before the chief priests, scribes, and elders, Jesus' witness is succinct and sure: I am the Christ, the Son of God (26:64): "In the future you will see the Son of Man sitting at the right hand of the Mighty One and coming on the clouds of heaven." Before Pilate our Lord is again succinct and sure (27:11): " 'Are You the king of the Jews?' 'Yes, it is as you say.' "

That phrase, *King of the Jews*, occurs again and again until it finally comes to rest at the top of the cross (27:37): "THIS IS JESUS, THE KING OF THE JEWS." Through St. Matthew's pen, God answers the question, "Is this Jesus of Nazareth really the Christ?"

Deuteronomy 18:21–22 said, "You may say to yourselves, 'How can we know when a message has not been spoken by the LORD?' If what a prophet proclaims in the name of the LORD does not take place or come true, that is a message the LORD has not spoken." Jesus' witness and Pilate's superscription answer the question, "What do you think of the Christ?" Jesus of Nazareth is the Christ. He has fulfilled the Scriptures.

He fulfills these words in His suffering (27:46): "My God, My God, why have You forsaken Me?" Jesus is abandoned, not only by Peter, by Judas, or by us in our sins, but He is abandoned by God Himself! What a mystery this is! The price of ransom for our sins is so great that God the Father forsakes His suffering Son! If people stand in awe before the Vietnam Memorial, consider the magnitude of what happened at Golgotha.

> *You who think of sin but lightly*
> *Nor suppose the evil great*
> *Here may view its nature rightly,*
> *Here its guilt may estimate.*
> *Mark the sacrifice appointed;*
> *See who bears the awful load;*
> *It's the Word, the Lord's Anointed,*
> *Son of Man and Son of God.*

Thomas Kelly, alt.

Conclusion: Our Constant Occupation

Display visual 8C from the CD-ROM.

Jesus Christ died for us and for our sins. No study, no lecture can ever touch the depth of what that solemn event means. We stand here on holy ground. Jesus' death is the constant occupation of our willing spirits, as we pray, as we worship, as we remember.

Concluding Activities

Distribute study leaflet 9 and encourage participants to read the article "Praying As Jesus Prayed" on pages 7–9 of the enrichment magazine.

Notes

The Resurrected Lord Sends Disciples with the Gospel

Matthew 28

Preparing for the Session

Central Focus

Everyone has a story to tell. The story of discipleship that we tell is a witness commissioned by our living and exalted Lord Jesus Christ.

Objectives

That the participant, as a child of God and with the Holy Spirit's help, will be led to

1. remember that not all know Jesus as the Messiah;
2. sharpen his or her witness to the historical resurrection of Jesus;
3. contrast the lowly Christ of earthly ministry to the same Christ in His exalted state;
4. learn some of the unique qualities of discipleship;
5. go and make disciples.

Note for small-group leaders: Lesson notes and other materials you will need begin on page 90.

For the Lecture Leader

You will probably find this lecture contains new and (we hope) interesting material. Acquaint yourself with it thoroughly. As you present the material on the resurrection, please remember and stress that the Holy Spirit working through the Word establishes faith in the resurrection. The arguments for the resurrection presented in the lecture are interesting, but they do not replace the witness of the Bible, nor do we verify what the Bible teaches by turning to extra-biblical sources.

As you present the final paragraphs on discipleship, deliver your material slowly. The mood at the end of this final lecture should be devotional. We have studied hard these weeks and learned much. We do not want to end with a classroom summary and a diploma of graduation. We do want to end with a greater love and devotion for Jesus, who fulfills God's promises to us and to all nations.

Session Plan

Worship

Ask participants to read silently the stanzas of the hymn printed in the study leaflet instead of singing them. While they do so, have your musician softly play the entire hymn (or use the music CD as accompaniment.) Then play the hymn again. This time have participants sing the stanzas. After the hymn have participants read the prayer in unison.

Devotion

Many communities celebrate "First Night" on December 31. Usually these events offer a safe and alcohol-free way to welcome in the new year. Matthew 28 tells the story of the "First Day"—the first day of the week, to be sure. But also the first day of our new lives in Christ. This day opened the door to eternal joy for us.

On Good Friday, Jesus' friends felt no joy. The tears of a few faithful followers watered the path to Joseph's garden tomb. That path looked, indeed, like the path toward disaster. That path ended where our lives here on earth will end too—at the cemetery. No place on earth looks bleaker than that! Try as we might, sin and Satan lead us down that garden path. They mean no good for us by it. Scripture itself calls death our "last enemy" (1 Corinthians 15:26).

But the garden path toward the tomb of our Lord did not dead-end in the grave. Jesus walked into death and through death. Then He emerged from the other side victorious, never to die again.

Our walk into death will not dead-end in the grave any more than did our Lord's. Because of what Jesus did for us during Holy Week, the garden path that leads us into the cemetery will also lead us back out from there and into life everlasting.

> *The sting of death is sin, and the power of sin is the law. But thanks be to God! He gives us the victory through our Lord Jesus Christ.*
>
> *Therefore, my dear brothers, stand firm. Let nothing move you. Always give yourselves fully to the work of the Lord, because you know that your labor in the Lord is not in vain.*

1 Corinthians 15:56–58

Lecture Presentation

This lecture also appears on the CD-ROM that accompanies this course. Also look at the PDFFILES directory on the CD-ROM for overhead transparency graphics for the course.

Introduction: Everyone Has a Story to Tell

Everyone has a story to tell. Centuries ago Jewish mothers in Europe would tell their children the "truth" about Jesus. Their story, told from generation to generation, was called the Tol'doth Yeshu. According to the Jewish scholar Joseph Klausner, one part of the story went like this:

> *The Sages of Israel recognized him [Jesus] and arrested him. They took and hanged him on the eve of Passover ... on a cabbage stem—for no other tree would bear him, because Yeshu [Jesus], during his lifetime, had adjured all trees by the "Ineffable Name" not to receive his body when he was hanged; but failed so to adjure the cabbage stem since that does not count as a tree. The body was taken down while it was yet the eve of the Sabbath (in order not to violate the prohibition: "His body shall not remain there for the night") and at once buried. But Yehuda the gardener removed the body from the tomb and cast it into a water-channel in the garden, and let the water flow over it as usual.*
>
> *When the disciples came and did not find the body in the tomb, they announced to the queen that Yeshu had been restored to life. The queen believed this.*

Joseph Klausner, *Jesus of Nazareth* (New York: The MacMillan Company, 1929), p. 50.

Everyone has a story to tell, but not every story is our story of discipleship, striding after the living Christ who calls out, "Follow Me." This lecture concludes our current Bible study series by reiterating one of St. Matthew's great purposes: witness. St. Matthew wrote his Gospel to tell the Jews that God had fulfilled His promises and sent the Messiah. The fulfillment of God's promises climaxes in the resurrection of the crucified Jesus and in the Lord's commission to tell the story to all nations.

1 The Historical Resurrection

About the resurrection ... The story we're commissioned to tell about Easter morning is a story that is historically true. The resurrection is an historical fact that is accepted by faith. Matthew 28:17 says, "When they saw Him [that is, the resurrected Christ], they worshiped Him; but some doubted." We need the Holy Spirit to believe and not to doubt the fact of the resurrection. There are, however, some very interesting historical facts about the resurrection that we disciples do well to know. These are facts that help sharpen our witness when we tell our story.

Display visuals 9A–9D from the CD-ROM as you work through the following points.

Consider these facts. First, the tomb was empty. The Tol'doth Yeshu with which we began our lecture acknowledged that the tomb was empty. That Jewish account said that "Yehuda the gardener removed the body from the tomb and cast it into a water-channel." That is reminiscent of John 20:15: Mary Magdalene "thinking He was the gardener ... said, 'Sir, if you have carried Him away, tell me where you have put Him.' " St. Matthew tells how the Jewish officials explained the empty tomb (28:12–14): "They gave the soldiers a large sum of money, telling them, 'You are to say, "His disciples came during the night and stole him away while we were asleep." ' "

My point is this: *Observers agreed that the tomb was empty. Either there was a theft of the body—or a real resurrection!*

Second, consider the change in Jesus' 11 disciples. They were not learned men. Acts 4:13 tells how the Sanhedrin was amazed at the witness of Peter and John, "when they ... realized that they were unschooled, ordinary men." And these ordinary men often disagreed and quarreled. Remember their argument about who is the greatest (18:1; 20:24, etc.)? Remember how they all ran away in Gethsemane? Do you think that such men could have fabricated this story, agreed on it through the years, and suffered martyrdom without one of them saying, "Oh, it was just a story. We made the whole thing up"?

Third, how shall we account for the rapid growth of the early church? Acts 2:47 says, "The Lord added to their number daily those who were being saved." Daily. Something must have happened to account for that kind of growth. I doubt that it was a new pastor or a slick evangelism program. That phenomenal growth is readily explained, though, by an historical resurrection and the subsequent appearances of Jesus Christ. Jesus strode out of His tomb—alive! And those who saw it could not be silenced by any threats or even death itself.

Fourth, an interesting passage appears in the writings of the Roman historian Tacitus. Tacitus, who lived in the late first and early second centuries after Christ, described Nero's persecution of Christians after the great fire at Rome:

> *All the endeavours of men, all the emperor's largesse and the propitiations of the gods, did not suffice to allay the scandal or banish the belief that the fire had been ordered. And so, to get rid of this rumour, Nero set up as the culprits and punished with the utmost refinement of cruelty a class hated for their abominations, who are commonly called Christians. Christus, from whom their name is derived, was executed at the hands of the procurator Pontius Pilate in the reign of Tiberius. Checked for the moment, this pernicious superstition again broke out, not only in Judaea, the source of the evil, but even in Rome.*

Tacitus, *Annales*, XV. 44. in *Documents of the Christian Church*, ed. Henry Bettenson (London: Oxford University Press, 1963).

Something happened after Christ was executed that made the so-called Christian "superstition" again break out. We know what that something was: the historical resurrection of Jesus Christ.

Fifth, a scholar named Pinchas Lapide wrote a fascinating book whose English title is *The Resurrection of Jesus: A Jewish Perspective*. Pinchas Lapide is not a Christian. He is, however, a Jewish scholar of the New Testament who believes that Jesus did rise from the dead. Let me say that again! Pinchas Lapide does not believe that Jesus is the Messiah but does believe that He rose from the dead. He says, "I accept the resurrection of Easter Sunday not as an invention of the community of disciples, but as a historical event" (*Jewish Monotheism and Christian Trinitarian Doctrine: A Dialogue by Pinchas Lapide and Jürgen Moltmann*, trans. Leonard Swidler [Philadelphia: Fortress Press, 1981]).

Now a lawyer might say that all this is circumstantial evidence. Fine. We don't need to discover the remnants of Noah's ark to believe in the historicity of the flood. Our belief in the resurrection is—finally—a matter of faith wrought by the Spirit through the Word. Remember Jesus' own words quoted by Luke (16:31): "If they do not listen to Moses and the Prophets, they will not be convinced even if someone rises from the dead." For us who believe that Jesus is the fulfillment of Moses and the Prophets, the evidences we have cited not only complement the Scriptural account, but they equip us to witness more effectively to "all nations."

2 The Exalted Lord

The story we have comes from one who has been resurrected—but there is more to the story than that. As Pinchas Lapide points out, a good number of people in both the Old and the New Testaments were brought back from the dead. Our commission comes from one who not only lives, but who has universal authority (28:18): "All authority in heaven and on earth has been given to Me."

Jesus made great claims, and people sensed an unusual authority in Him. Some examples:

> Matthew 9:6—"The Son of Man has authority on earth to forgive sins";
>
> Matthew 10:1—"He called His twelve disciples to Him and gave them authority to drive out evil spirits and to heal every disease and sickness";
>
> Matthew 7:29—"He taught as one who had authority, and not as their teachers of the law."

Those exercises of authority were usually limited. The Son of God did not invoke His divine prerogatives to make His earthly life easy. Even during the crucial days of Holy Week He said (Matthew 26:53-54): "Do you think I cannot call on My Father, and He will at once put at My disposal more than twelve legions of angels? But how then would the Scriptures be fulfilled that say it must happen in this way?" Jesus suffered all the way to abandonment by His Father.

But now Easter changes all. The Father raises His Son from the dead, indicating that the ransom for sins has been accepted (see 20:28). Contrast Jesus' limited exercise of authority during His state of humiliation with this sweeping statement: "All authority in heaven and on earth has been given to Me." This exalted authority of Christ is a splendid theme that glorifies our witness to all nations.

3 A Different Discipleship

Display visual 9E from the CD-ROM.

Jesus' authority forms the basis for the commission to tell our story—really, His story—to the world. In Matthew 28:19, He says, "Therefore, go and make disciples of all nations." Many pastors have had the experience of visiting an inactive member who asked, "Who sent you?" Our answer is quite simply Jesus Christ Himself! The Savior who has been given all authority bids us go to all nations and make disciples: *Make disciples.* Our commission is not simply to swell the rolls of the church or to have the most active congregation in town. Our commission is to make disciples, to have people confess, "The story of Jesus Christ is my story."

We invite people to a different kind of discipleship. It's different because we don't qualify our prospects before we tell the story. In Jesus' day you had to prove yourself qualified before you became the disciple of a rabbi. Jesus is different. The disciples He called were not qualified by the world's standards. Was Matthew the tax collector qualified? The religious establishment said no. Jesus calls the "unworthy" to discipleship. A fine cross-reference comes from St. Paul (1 Corinthians 1:26–29): "Brothers, think of what you were when you were called. Not many of you were wise by human standards; not many were influential; not many were of noble birth. But God chose the foolish things of the world to shame the wise; God chose the weak things of the world to shame the strong. He chose the lowly things of this world and the despised things—and the things that are not—to nullify the things that are, so that no one may boast before Him." When you go out to tell your story to make disciples, you don't have to qualify the prospects first! The story is for all nations.

We witness to a different kind of discipleship. In Jesus' day the bond between a rabbi and his disciples was the teaching. Jesus and His disciples are different. What bonds us to Jesus is Jesus. True, Jesus is known through His Word. Therefore, teaching and learning are an indispensable part of our discipleship, as we read in Matthew 28:19–20: "Make disciples of all nations … teaching them to obey everything I have commanded you." What the pagan Roman educator Quintilian said is also true for Christian disciples: "He must study always and everywhere" (*Institutio oratoria* X.7.26). But all the study and words must pass to the heart. The evidences of the resurrection, for example, are exciting to disciples because we believe that Jesus rose. Our teaching and learning is not a dry academic exercise but rather the result of an ardent love for our Savior. "Teaching them to obey everything I have commanded you." It's a very personal invitation, this call to discipleship.

There is nothing else beyond this discipleship. In Jesus' day a young man would have ambition beyond being the disciple of a rabbi. He would want to become a rabbi himself, an authority in his own right. So, discipleship was only a stage in life. Our commission to make disciples is different. There is an initiation, "baptizing them in the name of the Father and of the Son and of the Holy Spirit," but there is no graduation. As disciples of Jesus, we have arrived! We will, of course, continue to study and learn. Through Word and Sacrament our love for Him will grow. Greater sanctification (the ever more perfect soul) is our daily occupation. But we have no aspirations to graduate from discipleship. We simply want to be with Him always. "You are my portion, O LORD" (Psalm 119:57).

Conclusion: "I Am with You Always"

Jesus is always with us. Here's the conclusion to our Bible study (28:20): "Surely I am with you always, to the very end of the age." What a splendid fact with which we conclude! The risen and exalted Lord is with us. This is not the first assurance of His presence.

> Matthew 1:23—" 'They will call Him Immanuel'—which means, 'God with us.' "
>
> Matthew 18:20—"Where two or three come together in My name, there am I with them."

Now the inspired climax to us, His commissioned disciples: "I am with you always." Meditate on that. His ascension removed only His visible presence. "I am with you always," He promises. It's not just you and your afflictions, not just you and your joys, not just you and the people to whom you witness. "I am with you always," He says.

For the time being we now end our in-depth Bible study. We go our different ways, yet all of us travel the path of discipleship. Go, and know that the living and exalted Lord goes with you.

Concluding Activities

Make any necessary announcements, including information about the next LifeLight course. Encourage participants to read "Which Tomb?" and "Christ's Resurrection—A Fact of History" on pages 17–23 of the enrichment magazine.

Notes

Matthew Part 2

Small-Group Leaders Material

Growing as Faithful Disciples

Matthew 13:53–15:39

Preparing for the Session

Central Focus

This first session challenges the student to begin this course of in-depth Bible study with a desire for growth in faithful discipleship. The study should cause the student to look to Christ and the biblical Word for growth.

Objectives

That the participant, as a child of God and with the Holy Spirit's help, will be led to

1. verbalize a personal need for an increase in faith;
2. demonstrate that only Christ and His Word provide a reliable guide for life;
3. cast a critical eye at contemporary religious notions and their influence;
4. be encouraged by biblical demonstrations of faith.

For the Small-Group Leader

Your service as a discussion leader is about to begin. You can anticipate the joy of developing and deepening Christian friendships around God's Word in the weeks ahead.

You have received name tags for those who will be part of the small group you will lead. As your discussion group assembles, pass out the name tags. If the members of your group are unacquainted with one another, you may wish to play this enjoyable name game to help them learn names quickly in a way that will relax the tensions of a first meeting. (If group members are already known to one another, learning names will not be necessary, but the game may still be a great ice-breaker.)

To play the name game ask each participant to think of a positive adjective that begins with the same letter as his or her first name (Jovial Joe). Introduce yourself with such an adjective (Super Sam). Then ask the person at your left to repeat your adjective and name and add his or her own adjective and name. ("This is Super Sam, and I am Wonderful Wanda.") The next person repeats the previous two names before stating his or her own. The next person tries three besides his or her own. The game continues around the circle.

At the first meeting of your discussion group you may need to be especially patient and encouraging as the group comes to know one another and to settle in.

Small-Group Discussion Helps

Day 1 • Matthew 13:53–58

1. Jesus was about to begin the second phase of His public ministry. Before going on toward the cross, Jesus went home one more time. He had been absent for more than a year. People were probably eager to see Him again and hear what He had to say. Visiting rabbis were often invited to read and teach the Scriptures in the synagogue, and Jesus undoubtedly was invited to speak.

The people were amazed at what they heard. Jesus' words raised questions in their minds. They couldn't reconcile His wisdom and power with their preconceived notions of who Jesus was. Jesus and His family had lived among them. If their roots were the same, how could Jesus claim to be more than His neighbors and relatives? Such a claim was insulting and offensive. They rejected it. They refused to believe Jesus was the Messiah and expressed their derision and scorn in their questions.

The villagers name Jesus' brothers, but say nothing more about them. Other Gospel texts tell us Jesus' own family members refused to believe at this point. If anyone asks about this, point them to John 7:5. Later on

James became a leader in the church at Jerusalem and the author of the Book of James (Galatians 1:19; Acts 12:17; 15:13–19). Jude (Judas) also came to believe in Jesus and authored the book bearing his name (Jude).

Earlier in Jesus' ministry the people had become so angered by His claim to be the Messiah, His condemnation of Israel, and His favorable attitude toward the Gentiles that they drove Him from the synagogue and were ready to kill Him.

Jesus was not surprised that the people refused to change their minds about Him. Nevertheless, He offered them a second chance.

2. (a) Pride stood in the way. To the people in Nazareth Jesus was no different than they. Jesus understood this (v. 57). (b) In contrast, the Samaritans welcomed Jesus and begged Him to stay with them. They listened to Jesus and came to believe He was the Savior of the world!

3. The unbelieving attitude of the people at Nazareth raised a barrier that made it impossible for Jesus to have any effect on them. Jesus did not perform miracles in such a climate of unbelief, and He marveled at their lack of faith.

4. (a) Indifference, self-sufficiency, a desire to handle things on our own, refusal to recognize our need, self-indulgence, anxiety—all create barriers to the trust Jesus seeks to nurture in our hearts. (b) Faith in Jesus is His gift to us. He seeks an open heart, a humble mind, an expectant spirit where He may plant the seeds of faith and help them grow, where the Holy Spirit may level every barrier.

Day 2 • Matthew 14:1–12

5. Herod appears confused, frightened, and plagued by a guilty conscience. He knew John spoke the truth about his sin. Murdering John could not quiet Herod's guilt.

6. (a) Herod was shocked, conscience-stricken, easily influenced, and afraid. Both Herod and Herodias were unfaithful, morally weak, selfish, and self-centered. Herodias was vindictive, manipulative, and jealous. She taught Salome to be seductive, leaving her morally weak. She used Salome. John was faithful, frank, and courageous. His disciples grieved over John's death. (b) Ask group members for other insights into the characters in this text.

Day 3 • Matthew 14:13–36

7. Jesus accepted the situation, welcomed the people, and used this opportunity to show His love and care through healing, teaching, and eventually, feeding.

8. (a) The weary disciples would have dismissed the hungry crowd, leaving them on their own. When Jesus challenged them to solve the problem, the disciples used a practical eye to evaluate their resources, compare them to the requirements, and tally the expense. They concluded, "It can't be done!" (b) Jesus, however, couples the meager resources at hand with His blessing, and the impossible happens.

9. (a) All day long the crowd had experienced Jesus' acceptance, His compassion, His loving touch, His encouraging words. Surely they were joyfully expectant, trusting in His love for them, while at the same time not knowing exactly what would happen. The huge crowd arranged themselves in groups with women and children separated from the men as the Jewish custom of the time dictated.

(b) After the meal everyone was satisfied. The Jews believed bread was a gift of God and were required to save scraps. Gratefully the people helped fill the small flask-shaped wicker baskets (actually lunch boxes) each disciple carried as part of his standard gear. (Maybe the disciples ate the leftovers for lunch the next day!)

(c) Point out that we remain expectant because we trust Jesus' abiding love for us—even when we don't know for sure what will happen next and even when we repeatedly fail Jesus. Stress the importance of having faith in Jesus' love for us personally.

10. Allow for personal responses. Jesus may have thanked His Father for the blessings of the miracle. He may have prayed for those who misunderstood His mission and ministry. He may have communed with His Father about the turn in direction His ministry was taking.

11. Jesus knew the disciples were in need. They couldn't handle the storm alone. Jesus came quickly and directly to their aid—walking across the water. With Him they would be secure.

12. (a) Peter looked away from Jesus to assess the storm's strength. When he did, Peter's doubt caused him to sink. (b) More important than Peter's doubt, however, was Jesus' saving act. (c) Jesus held Peter (not the reverse). How often Jesus' loving touch (note the use of touch in vv. 35–36) is seen in the Gospels—as He accepts, helps, heals, rescues. Jesus acts quickly, personally, effectively with us too. He responds graciously even to the prayers of those of little faith.

Day 4 • Matthew 15:1–20

13. A fact-finding delegation of scribes and Pharisees came to Jesus at Gennesaret to ask Him an important question. They were determined to find out where He stood on the basic religious traditions which they held sacred and binding. Because the religious rules affected every aspect of the daily life of the Jews, the religious leaders enjoyed immense power over the people. If Jesus contradicted this tradition, what would happen to their position and authority in the community? The leaders approached Jesus personally to find the answer.

14. (a) Jesus asked the scribes and Pharisees why they broke God's commands in order to keep their traditions. The basic question was, "Which is more important—God's Word or man's tradition adding to what God's Word means?" (b) Jesus contrasts the words "Honor your father and your mother" in Exodus 20:12 and 21:17 with the Pharisees' interpretation of Numbers 30:1–2. Jesus rejects their practice of using one biblical teaching to nullify another. He shows how their traditions adhere to the letter of the Law while ignoring its spirit. (c) In verses 8–9 Jesus quotes Isaiah 29:13. The scribes and Pharisees had used ritual to ease their consciences. Jesus accuses them of substituting their rules for God's teachings, of offering God cold hearts and empty lip service.

15. Jesus emphasizes that sin begins in the human heart. True defilement comes from an impure heart—not from a violation of external rules. It's not what we eat, but what we think, desire, and speak that defiles us and makes us unfit for worship and fellowship with God and one another.

16. (a) The disciples saw that the Lord's words had offended the powerful Pharisees. Perhaps the disciples were afraid the Pharisees would make trouble and interfere with their ministry. (b) Jesus points out that the Pharisees and their traditions are not "planted" by God but are pulled up and dead. Jesus warns the disciples to ignore the Pharisees' teaching and refuse to follow them to their death.

Day 5 • Matthew 15:21–39

17. (a) The deep love for her child drove this Gentile mother to seek out Jesus, resting privately in a home near Tyre. Some from that region had been in the crowds witnessing His earlier miracles (Mark 3:8), and now the mother sees Jesus as her only hope. She cries, she begs, she humbly expresses her needs, and accepts God's grace as a beggar, praying from "under the table." She refuses to be discouraged. While some in your group may see Jesus' words here as harsh and uncaring, it is perhaps best to let the outcome speak for itself. The Lord's words did not drive the woman away. Rather, she answered each of His remarks with a comeback indicating stronger confidence in His goodness. As the woman's God and Savior, Jesus knew exactly how she would respond. While you or I may have responded differently, falling into outrage or despair, she did not. If participants ask about Jesus' brusque manner, point them to His wisdom and the final results of this encounter.

(b) When Jesus reviews God's purpose in sending the Savior first to the Jews, the woman submits to letting God act in His own way—that is, through Israel to the world (Matthew 10:6; John 4:22–23; Romans 1:16–17). Jesus awakens this woman's faith, rejoices at being received, worshiped, and understood by a Gentile woman, and then opens His treasure to her, assuring her she can have what she wants! In this incident Jesus was also teaching His disciples that He intends salvation for the Gentiles too.

18. Jesus' primary objective for us is that we learn to trust Him. More important than health, security, safety, and happiness is the faith Jesus desires to give us. In the end our faith is all that matters. Sometimes, as in the case of this Canaanite woman, Jesus withholds an immediate answer to prayer in order to give us the greater blessing of a stronger faith.

19. While the feeding of the 5,000 appears in all four Gospels, the feeding of the 4,000 is found only in Matthew and Mark. In both cases the meal was preceded by Jesus' compassionate healing. Because it took place in Gentile territory, the feeding of the 4,000 probably involved more Gentiles, which accounts for Matthew's explanation at the end of verse 31. The 5,000 were fed in spring when the grass was green; the 4,000 in summer when the ground was dry and bare. In both accounts Jesus tested the disciples; they acknowledged the inadequate food supply; the crowd had been with Jesus for three days; He had them sit down; He prayed to the Father; the disciples participated in the distribution. The seven baskets in the latter account may have been large hampers used by the Gentiles.

20. (a) Note that Jesus Himself is the Bread of life (John 6:25–59) and that He comes to us in His body and blood in the Sacrament and in His holy Word. (b) It's not enough to admire these gifts—they must be consumed, becoming part of our very selves, energizing our will. Without His food we sicken and die. (c) Talk about ways to share Jesus, the Bread of life, with others. Plan specific ways to do this.

21. Use this question to give persons in the group an opportunity to share and to ask questions still unanswered. Perhaps the group as a whole can help with remaining questions or you can follow up. Don't forget to end the session with a brief prayer. Thank God for the insights that have been gained.

Notes

Small-Group Leaders Session 2 — **Matthew Part 2**

To Glory through the Cross

Matthew 16–17

Preparing for the Session

Central Focus

The First Commandment, "You shall have no other gods before Me," is more easily recited than lived. This session examines discipleship as self-denial and suffering with the hope of glory.

Objectives

That the participant, as a child of God and with the Holy Spirit's help, will be led to

1. understand the true nature of Israel's Messiah;
2. feel overwhelmed but all the more called to a life of self-denial;
3. leave glory to the future and fill the present with the concern of discipleship.

For the Small-Group Leader

As the leader of your discussion group, your attention will be focused in two places. First you will focus on the Word of God that your group is studying together. Members of your group probably are taking part in Life-Light because they want to study God's Word. They want to know that Word better. They want it to have a greater part in their lives. You are helping guide them as they do that. Together your group is making the Word of God its primary focus.

But the individual people who are members of your group provide another focus for you and for each member of your group. These individuals are bringing themselves to God through His Word because they realize they have certain needs they want that Word to address. At times study questions will encourage the group members to surface those needs. Help the members of your group apply the Word to those specific needs that become apparent. Be sensitive and caring, and you will set a positive example to others in your group in this regard.

Make prayer a part of your group meetings. Not only at the end of the discussion period, but also at other times you may wish to invite the group to speak to the Lord in prayer, perhaps regarding a particular need of one or more members of your group.

Day 1 • Matthew 16:1–12

1. Jesus' opponents demanded He give them a spectacular sign, a special revelation just for them. They wanted to test and trick Jesus, to dictate on what terms they would accept Him. They were manipulative and unwilling to repent. They claimed to belong to God, yet they were unfaithful to Him. Jesus refused to comply, calling them wicked and adulterous, and offering the sign of Jonah. (See Jesus' explanation in 12:40.) In chapter 16 the Sadducees team up with the Pharisees. The Sadducees were a Jewish party, usually opponents of the Pharisees. They were few in number but well educated, wealthy, and powerful. Although they claimed to follow the written Word of God alone, in reality they favored the thinking of the Greeks, neglecting Jewish custom and tradition. They conducted political affairs, ruled the Sanhedrin, and one of them, Caiaphas, proposed the death of Jesus (John 11:49–53; 18:14). Here the Sadducees join the Pharisees to harass Jesus.

The Pharisees and Sadducees had rejected the clear signs already given in Jesus' miracles that identified Him as God's Son and the promised Messiah. These were the signs of the times the Pharisees and Sadducees could not read. God's sign was Jesus Himself. Perhaps this is why Jesus sadly turned away and left them to their unbelief. (Note Matthew 27:41–43.)

2. (a) The influence of the teachings of the Pharisees and Sadducees was still on Jesus' mind as He and the disciples set out across the lake. The effects of such influence on the disciples' faith was uppermost in His mind, for His primary objective was that the disciples know and trust Him. (b) The disciples were preoccu-

pied with food for the body, while Jesus was concerned about food for their faith.

3. (a) The corrupting influence of the Pharisees was their emphasis on keeping outward rules (the letter of the Law) while ignoring the state of the heart (the spirit of the Law). Such an emphasis ultimately leads to self-reliance and self-righteousness and a turning away from God's mercy and forgiveness. The Sadducees' concerns with materialism and political power were also dangerous influences. Jesus taught that the Kingdom is not concerned with amassing and protecting earthly goods, nor does that Kingdom come through political action. Jesus warns the disciples to beware of these influences. (b) Remembering how Jesus had miraculously fed the multitudes would encourage the disciples to trust their Lord for all they would need—beginning with their righteousness before God.

Day 2 • Matthew 16:13–20

4. (a) Some people believed Jesus was John the Baptizer, Elijah, or Jeremiah returned from the dead. (b) Let participants comment. While some unbelievers peg Jesus as a fool or a fraud, many people will express respect for Jesus as a great teacher. However, they ignore the fact that Jesus, in fact, claimed to be God Incarnate. If He lied, then how could He be "a great teacher"? Christians believe Jesus' claim to deity. We know Jesus as true God, true man, the Son of God and our Savior from sin.

5. (a) Peter confessed, "You are the Christ, the Son of the living God." *Christ* is Greek for "the Anointed One." In Hebrew the word is *Messiah*. Kings were anointed. Peter was recognizing Jesus as God's Messiah, the deliverer of the Jews, and his Lord and King. (b) Jesus calls for a personal response from the disciples (and us) for faith is our personal link to Jesus (Mark 16:16; John 3:16, 18, 36; 2 Corinthians 13:5). Our life depends on that link. (c) Encourage members to share their personal "confessions" of Christ.

6. There is an important progression of thought in Jesus' response to Peter's confession. (a) Simon Peter's earthly father could not reveal Christ to him—only the heavenly Father could give Peter that revelation (John 1:10–13). (b) A foundation, even one made of rocks, cannot be laid on shifting ground. It must be laid upon solid bedrock. God, in Christ Jesus, is the rock on which His church is built. (c) Christ is the cornerstone that holds the church together (Ephesians 2:19–20). The apostles, expressing their faith in their witness and teachings, constitute the foundation (together with the prophets). In this fundamental role of establishing the church, the apostles play the role of servants, not lords. (d) Everyone who shares Peter's confession of Christ in faith also shares his role as servant and becomes another living stone added to His church (1 Peter 2:4–10). (e) Satan's "biggest gun" is physical death. He uses it to threaten and frighten God's children. But Jesus promises that nothing, not even death, will be able to hold Christ or His church. In Christ's Easter triumph, death is swallowed up in victory (1 Corinthians 15:54–57). (f) **Challenge question.** Jesus gave Peter and the apostles the authority to announce forgiveness to the penitent and judgment to the unrepentant. Those who reject the Gospel are bound under the judgment of God. Those who believe the Gospel are set free from sin and death. (g) Jesus clearly gave this authority, not only to Peter, but to the other apostles and to the entire church.

Day 3 • Matthew 16:21–28

7. (a) Peter believed in Jesus as the Messiah, but it was hard for him to fully comprehend the implications of that belief. Peter's idea of a Messiah was a victorious king, not a Suffering Servant. Peter's love for Jesus, his vision, his plans for the future, even his fear may have caused him to rebuke Jesus. (b) Human reason sees no victory in death, only defeat. Human reason rejects suffering and seeks safety, advantage, and ease.

8. Jesus reminds us that those who would be His disciples will sacrifice their will to do His will, become obedient, be ready to spend themselves for others, and allow Him to lead. Luke writes this will be done daily (Luke 9:23).

9. Some authorities believe this verse is fulfilled in the transfiguration (17:1–3). Note Peter's explanation in 2 Peter 1:16–18. The transfiguration was for Peter, James, and John a foretaste of Jesus' glorious Second Coming—a hint of the resurrection and Pentecost.

Matthew Part 2 — Small-Group Leaders Session 2

Day 4 • Matthew 17:1–13

10. (a) The glory of the Son of God was revealed. His glory, though hidden now on earth, would be revealed fully when He returned. (b) Moses, the lawgiver and deliverer from bondage, represented the old covenant and the promise of salvation. Elijah, the appointed restorer of all things (Malachi 4:5–6), represented the prophets, preparing the way for the Messiah. The transfiguration confirms Jesus as the Messiah, who fulfills the Law and the Prophets through His death and resurrection. Moses, Elijah, and Jesus discussed His impending death and resurrection (Luke 9:30–31), which would bring God's people out of bondage and restore them to God.

Moses' work was finished by Joshua (which means "the Lord saves"). Elijah's work was finished by Elisha, a form of *Joshua*. Jesus, also a form of *Joshua*, finished the work of both by bringing their work to fulfillment. The greatest lawgiver and the greatest prophet recognized and acknowledged Jesus as the one whom they foretold. What encouragement that must have given Jesus!

11. (a) At first the disciples seem unaware and inattentive. It may have been night. They may have been sleepy (Luke 9:32), groggy, and frightened by what they saw (Mark 9:6). Matthew says they were terrified. Without thinking, Peter inappropriately suggests he put up booths or tents so they might all remain in Christ's transfigured presence.

(b) Later Peter rested his message on what he heard and saw at the transfiguration and on the testimony of Scripture. His message did not come from human imagination, but from God. His experience on the mountain confirmed this, shaping and strengthening his ministry. We can assume it had a similar affect on the other disciples.

12. Perhaps Jesus wanted the disciples to keep silent until they fully understood, after the resurrection, what kind of Messiah He is. Perhaps until His work on the cross was completed He wanted no one and nothing to stand in the way of His journey toward that goal.

13. Jesus explains that Elijah must come first as the teachers of the law correctly assert—and that "Elijah" has already returned, John the Baptizer having assumed Elijah's prophetic mantle of authority.

Day 5 • Matthew 17:14–27

14. (a) Returning from the mountain, Jesus immediately meets a desperate father with a need. Human need never ends. Yet the father needs something even greater than the expulsion of a demon. He needs Jesus to create and nurture faith within his heart. This is Jesus' first priority (Mark 9:21–25). Jesus teaches the father to trust Him.

(b) The disciples must learn the same lesson. Although they had received the power to cast out demons (10:1), they failed because they placed their trust in themselves (v. 19). They had forgotten their power over demonic spirits came from Jesus. He reminds them that faith works through prayer (Mark 9:29). And Jesus assures them that even the most limited faith can "move mountains" by laying hold of the whole power of God.

(c) This faith trusts not in faith and not in human ability. Instead, it focuses on Christ's love and power.

15. Before his death Moses sang the song in Deuteronomy 32. Jesus echoes Moses. We might point to the materialism, sexual permissiveness, condoning of abortions, the growing acceptance of euthanasia, and many other evidences of the widespread unbelief that characterizes our own generation.

16. (a) Perhaps Jesus hoped the disciples would trust Him enough to accept what He told them about His coming death and resurrection even though they couldn't fully understand it. Perhaps He hoped they would wait patiently and expectantly and rejoice at the promise that He would be raised to life. (b) Matthew says the disciples grieved; Mark writes they were confused and afraid.

17. (a) A Jew who refused to pay the temple tax looked like an overt atheist. Other Jews wouldn't even begin to listen to the Gospel preached by one who refused this obligation. Even though Jesus points out that He and the disciples belong to God's royal household and are exempt from the tax, nevertheless they will pay so as not to cause anyone to stumble on their account. (b) Jesus' love motivates all who follow Christ.

18. Permit group members to share insights and questions from their study. Don't forget to conclude the session with a prayer. Ask the Holy Spirit to enable us to acknowledge Jesus as the Christ.

Helping Disciples Restore an Erring Brother

Matthew 18

Preparing for the Session

Central Focus

The quality of our life with God and with one another requires that we give careful attention to the welfare of one another's soul. The song that says "they are precious in His sight; Jesus loves the little children of the world" is true of all disciples. This session is about how we demonstrate it in our relationships with one another.

Objectives

That the participant, as a child of God and with the Holy Spirit's help, will be led to

1. take greater care not to cause others to sin;
2. gain a more accurate understanding of the steps for dealing with sin outlined in Matthew 18;
3. think of discipleship less as an individual pursuit and more as a group concern.

For the Small-Group Leader

As discussion leader, one of your tasks is to pace the progress of discussing the questions for the week. While there may be times when the group will not be able to discuss all of the study questions, most of the time you should make your way through all of the questions.

Each session includes 30 to 35 questions. In a 55-minute discussion period there will be approximately one and one-half minutes for each question. While some questions will require more time to answer and others will require less, knowing how much time is available for each question should help you keep track of how you are doing.

As you plan each discussion session you may want to decide which questions will receive greater emphasis and which less so you may allow time accordingly.

Small-Group Discussion Helps

Day 1 • Matthew 18:1–9

1. (a) Jesus clearly states that whoever humbles himself or herself like a trusting and unpretentious child is the greatest in His kingdom (v. 4). Just as a child is dependent on parents, unaware of rank or position, and is unconscious of being humble, so also members of Christ's kingdom lean upon the heavenly Father and are open to His direction. Through word and example Jesus taught that greatness is found in service.

(b) The disciples seem to ignore all this teaching about greatness in service. They also ignore Jesus' talk about the cross. They think only of themselves. Their self-serving nature leads to arguments. Their proud, boastful, domineering self-assertiveness must be changed. Life in the Kingdom involves service, not power.

(c) Jesus doesn't criticize the disciples for wanting to be great, but for their warped idea of greatness. Perhaps the disciples scorned the work of teaching children (19:13) or despised the "little people" of this world who have no status, authority, or power (15:23), or were concerned about making the right impressions on the "big people" (15:12). Jesus turns things around. He values children, including toddlers and babies. Jesus also values "newborn Christians," still in the process of growing. It was also not uncommon for a rabbi to refer to his own disciples as his little children.

2. (a) Let participants comment. Open sin, off-hand remarks, acrid criticism—we can subvert the faith of the childlike believer in any one of a hundred ways. We pray that God will guard our lips and our lives so that we never commit the sins against which our Lord here warns. (b) No punishment is too great for those who hurt the childlike. Drowning in the depths of the sea indicated utter destruction and annihilation. The large millstone pulled by a donkey in grinding grain contrasted with the smaller one used daily in the household. Jesus' mention of the "millstone" shows the grav-

Matthew Part 2 — Small-Group Leaders Session 3

ity of the sin and the weight of God's condemnation.

3. There is nothing more important than faith. No sacrifice is too costly to avoid hurting the "children" in our midst or causing them to lose their faith.

Day 2 • Matthew 18:10–14

4. (a) In verses 1–9 Jesus has identified the "little ones" as His followers who may be young in years, new in the faith, or childlike in their humility and unpretentiousness. In verse 10 Jesus instructs the disciples (potential leaders in His church) to be careful not to view these "little ones" with disdain, (b) because each of them is very precious to the Father—so precious that their angels have constant access to the Father, who will search for and rescue any one of them who wanders off. The Bible tells us that angels serve God also by serving Christians, especially in matters regarding their salvation. For references to the way in which angels serve Christians see Psalm 34:7; 91:11; and Hebrews 1:14.

5. Encourage members to describe in their own words the heavenly Father pictured for them in Jesus' parable. Note the love of the Father for individuals whom He refuses to write off. He loves even the foolish, rebellious, and thickheaded as individuals. The Father is patient. While we may be unwilling to "waste" sympathy on a fool, He is not. He seeks and searches; He loves. The Father rejoices; He is happy to reclaim His own.

6. (a) and (b) Knowing how much God values sinners affects our attitude toward ourselves and others. We experience the love of God, refrain from degrading ourselves, honestly confess our own sins, and are assured of God's forgiveness. We experience peace instead of fear. We are more accepting of others and assure them of God's eagerness to forgive by our own readiness to forgive.

Day 3 • Matthew 18:15–20

7. (a) The brother (or sister) is a fellow believer. The term *brother* is used here for the first time; it describes loving relationships in God's family. Here Jesus makes it clear the church must be concerned for her "sheep" who stumble. (b) The motivation for confrontation is love. The motivation must be to turn the offender to repentance—not to prove the accuser right or extract payment for the wrong.

8. Jesus provides a structure necessary for love to operate. He describes three steps for winning back the erring one. First go directly to the person who has sinned and discuss the matter privately. Next invite someone else to assist in the process of reconciliation. Then discuss the matter with the fellowship of believers. When reconciliation is not possible the erring one may be released from fellowship, is no longer considered a brother or sister, and assumes a different role.

9. (a) Jesus treated Gentiles and tax collectors with a love that sought to win them through repentance and forgiveness to faith. (b) Although the brother or sister who has sinned and broken fellowship with other believers may no longer be within the fellowship—still no one is to be counted utterly hopeless. Jesus challenges us to win him or her with His kind of love, love that can touch the hardest heart.

10. Harmony in the fellowship of believers is Jesus' goal. The entire church is affected spiritually by conflict, losing spiritual oneness and power. Reconciliation is important because great power is promised to those who agree—their prayers are answered, and Jesus Himself is present.

Day 4 • Matthew 18:21–35

11. (a and b) The church is a family of the forgiven. This truth is reflected in Jesus' parable of the unmerciful servant. The main teaching of the parable is this: Forgive! Peter wanted to put legal limits on his forgiveness, but Jesus tells him to forgive without stopping to keep count.

12. The king ordered the indebted servant, his wife, children, and all he owned to be sold to repay the debt, a practice familiar to Jesus' listeners. Servitude as a means of debt payment was permitted in the Old Testament law. The king had justice on his side.

13. (a) The servant was terrified. He fell to his knees. He did not acknowledge his debt—only begged for

patience. (b) He made a rash promise to repay everything he owed. He had to know this was impossible. How could someone hope to repay $15 million, more than 10 times the yearly income of a king? Yet he claimed the ability to do it. (c) The king gives more than the servant asks. The servant asks for patience, for time to pay; the king freed him from any obligation to pay—ever. The debt was canceled. (d) We might expect such mercy to produce thanks, love, joy, compassion—yet not one of these is evident.

14. (a) The servant found his fellow servant. (b) The debt owed the forgiven servant was tiny compared to the debt he had been forgiven. (c) Yet the plea is the same: "Be patient with me." Answers will vary as to the servant's lack of mercy for his fellow servant. Accept reasonable responses.

15. (a) The king expected the forgiven servant to imitate the king's example by showing a similar mercy to his fellow servant. (b) In anger the king condemned the unmerciful servant to suffer until he had paid his own debt in full.

Day 5 • Matthew 18:21–35

16. (a) The unmerciful servant asked for patience; that suggests that he desired mercy. But he also claimed to be able to pay the entire debt by himself. That suggests he felt he could satisfy the king with justice. (b) When it came to dealing with his fellow servant, however, the first servant was unwilling to consider mercy at all. (c) Our fallen human nature wants to assert that we can satisfy God's justice. Sinful pride and self-righteousness convince us that it's possible to please God on our own. Humility born of the Spirit leads us to throw ourselves on God's mercy. In humble faith we accept the payment Jesus made of our debt.

17. The trifling debt others owe us becomes so hard to forgive when we set ourselves in God's place, when we ignore the enormity of our own debt, and when we may not have truly experienced the mercy of God ourselves. Like the unmerciful servant we may reject God's mercy by failing to do the following: admit our own need, come to God humbly, and allow His mercy to reach deep within our hearts.

18. We may smugly feel justified in refusing to forgive until the offender meets certain conditions. Lead participants to put the message of the parable into their own words. Some may be willing to share a specific situation where they feel God is calling them to forgive freely, unconditionally, from their hearts.

19. Encourage group members, as time permits, to share insights, reaffirmed convictions, or unanswered questions. Conclude with a prayer that praises God for His grace and asks for help in forgiving others.

Notes

Small-Group Leaders Session 4 — Matthew Part 2

Preparing Disciples to Trust in God's Grace

Matthew 19–20

Preparing for the Session

Central Focus

Childlike trust in God and service to others are the qualities of following Christ. This session brings those virtues home against the backdrop of calculating self-interest.

Objectives

That the participant, as a child of God and with the Holy Spirit's help, will be led to

1. ask God to grant them childlike trust in Christ;
2. learn to abhor egotistical self-interest;
3. act in Christlike and childlike ways in all relationships;
4. be awed by God's grace.

For the Small-Group Leader

One of your goals as a small-group leader is to encourage a discussion group in which each participant is able to take part and contribute as he or she desires and needs. Clearly, these desires and needs will vary among participants. Some will speak more, others less. The level of participation for each person will also vary from one session to the next. Your goal is not to see that each participant speaks no more or less than others, but to see that each participant has an equal opportunity to take part in the group over the nine sessions of this course.

Fulfilling this goal will take some sensitivity and tact on your part. You will want to be aware of and sensitive to each member of your group—the quieter ones as well as the more talkative members. This awareness and sensitivity on your part will go a long way toward achieving the goal.

As the small-group leader you will be able to open the way for the participants who are more shy or insecure.

"Let's hear how George responded to this question." Of course you will want to be sure that "George" actually wants to share his answer or to say something. If you are uncertain about this, ask "George" at another time whether he would like an opportunity to speak more frequently. Or ask the members of the group to signal by raising their hands slightly if they wish to respond or speak. In this way you will be able to call upon participants in a more equitable manner.

Small-Group Discussion Helps

Day 1 • Matthew 19:1–15

1. (a) Jesus' enemies pursue Him toward the cross. He goes willingly in obedience to the Father's will; yet on the way He suffers taunts and attempts from others to trap and alienate Him from those who listen and follow.

(b) The Pharisees knew their question about divorce was controversial. Not everyone could agree on justifiable reasons for divorce. Even the rabbis differed on their interpretation of Deuteronomy 24:1–4. Shammai taught that the "something indecent" a husband found in his wife referred only to marital unfaithfulness, the one allowable cause for divorce. Hillel taught that if a wife becomes "displeasing" to her husband, he had grounds for divorce—if he came to dislike her, if she burned his food, if he desired another, or if she was disrespectful to their parents. The Pharisees intended to trap Jesus into opposing the popular view of Hillel and to set the majority of the people against Him. Jesus pointed to God's original intent for marriage.

2. (a) Marriage is intended for procreation (Genesis 1:27–28) and companionship (Genesis 2:18). It is to be a close, insoluble union (Genesis 2:23–25), where mutual submission, Christlike self-sacrificing love, commitment, care, and respect are expressed (Eph-

esians 5:21–33) for a lifetime (1 Corinthians 7:39). God had created one man and one woman for each other and joined them in a sacred union of His design intended to meet the deepest of human needs. Every marriage thus joined by God is sacred to Him. The married couple were created for God and each other. They are His special possession. Therefore, in principle, any division or destruction of what belongs to God is sinful. Then, too, marriage pictures Christ's relationship with His Bride, the church. As Christ will never leave His Bride, neither should earthly husbands desert their wives.

(b) Jesus corrects the Pharisees by pointing out that Moses did not command divorce. Divorce was a temporary concession to the hardness of human hearts. It was allowed out of mercy for women who, without it, would be discarded without provision. (Women had few legal rights. Nevertheless, unless a woman was a notorious sinner, her dowry must be returned to her if she were divorced by her husband.) Note God's reaction to divorce in Malachi 2:13–16. Here and in Matthew 5:31–32 marital unfaithfulness is grounds for divorce. Malicious desertion, rather than a cause for divorce, is in itself divorce.

(c) The disciples conclude that if marriage is such a sacred binding, if divorce is hated by God, if the risks are so great, then it's better not to marry at all! Not everyone can accept the binding nature of marriage. Only those who have the continual help of Jesus and the guidance of the Holy Spirit will build a relationship in marriage that God's ideal demands. Furthermore, marriage is not God's best gift for every person—as Jesus points out in verses 11–12. As you work through this question emphasize the importance of living according to our calling, whether married or single.

(d) Point out that in this section Jesus wants us to understand the true nature of marriage and the importance of entering into marriage carefully. Be sure participants are clear on the Gospel's message of forgiveness for all who repent. And help them realize that we should not despise, pressure, or pity those who never marry. Note, too, that the lecture will address the issues raised by this set of questions. If, after the lecture, questions remain unanswered, urge participants to talk them over with your pastor. Or offer to research the questions and report back next time.

3. It can't be a coincidence that these verses (13–15) describing Jesus' blessing of the children follow the section on marriage and divorce. It was always Jesus' desire to conserve life, the family, children. Divorce fractures all these. Encourage group members to think of ways parents may selfishly hinder their children's faith.

Day 2 • Matthew 19:16–30

4. (a) The man in this text was rich, a ruler of a synagogue, probably a Pharisee, earnest and intent on living up to what was expected of him. He thinks in terms of righteousness based on works.

(b) Since he attempts to relate to God on the basis of his own goodness, he can never be sure he is good enough. Jesus reminds him God alone is good and that all goodness is derived from Him.

5. Jesus holds up the mirror of the Law to show the man his basic sin of self-interest or self-love. When pressed to be more specific, Jesus points to the second table of the Ten Commandments, summarized in "love your neighbor as yourself." (See Leviticus 19:18 and Matthew 22:37–40.)

6. (a) Jesus does not ask every Christian to sell all possessions and give them to the poor. God may also give wealth as a blessing. But Jesus does require that we love no one or nothing else more than we love and serve Him. Jesus' command here was designed to show this young man the tight grip possessions had on his heart. While he may well have outwardly obeyed many of the commandments to love his neighbors, he crassly disobeyed the prohibition against trusting other gods. His possessions were his idols, and Jesus tried to show him that.

(b) Perhaps this man had a family to provide for. Perhaps he had worked very hard to achieve the wealth and financial success he possessed. Perhaps in his mind creature comforts had become necessities. Perhaps his self-esteem and social position were closely linked to his possessions. The cost of giving it all up to follow Jesus was just too great. He could not love his neighbor that much for he loved himself more. In an effort to conserve what he had, he lost everything—eternal life, companionship with Jesus, true security, fulfillment—and joy (v. 22).

7. (a) Verse 26 is a key verse here. Only God's grace is able to save us from the powerful grip of self-centeredness, materialism, idolatry. If only the rich man had admitted his helplessness and asked for Jesus' mercy and power! All are saved by grace, through faith.

(b) Our sinful nature is only too ready to substitute another god (such as our possessions) for the true God. The Law constantly scrutinizes us and calls us to repentance. A continual exposure to the mirror of God's Law is necessary to drive us to the Gospel, where we find forgiveness and cleansing.

8. God will provide for those who have renounced for His sake the blessings of this world, giving much more abundant and more excellent blessings "at the renewal of all things" when we will "inherit eternal life."

Day 3 • Matthew 20:1–16

9. (a) The vineyard was the landowner's; he had the right to manage it his way. (b) The owner offered a denarius. He promised to pay what was right. (c) The workers were called into the vineyard at different times, some early, some at midday, others late, because the landowner found them at different times. (d) The workers hired first expected payment based on merit—according to their own logic and values. (e) They grumbled and accused the landowner of unfairness. They found fault with his gracious generosity. (f) The landowner exhibits incredible patience and love, addressing the complainer as "Friend," yet correcting his faulty thinking. He helps him recognize his real problems—envy, jealousy, and questioning the landowner's grace.

10. First, consider the point of the parable. The vineyard represents the kingdom of heaven; the landowner, God. The laborers are all who have heard the Gospel call. The day is that period of grace from creation until Christ's Second Coming. (The hours of the day represent different points in this time period or different times in life when an individual hears and heeds the Gospel call.) The payment is clearly not a wage paid for work accomplished, but a gift given purely out of grace since all receive the same regardless of the length of service or what was endured. This gift is eternal life. The main point is that God's gracious promise of eternal life is the same for all who believe and is much more than anyone has merited. Remind one another that it is only by grace through faith that anyone receives eternal life; salvation is not the reward for living a "good" life on earth. Note God's graciousness in continuing to call workers into His vineyard. He wants all to be saved. Can we afford to be less gracious than God?

Day 4 • Matthew 20:17–28; Mark 10:32–34; Luke 18:31–33

11. This third prediction of Jesus' suffering and death in verses 17–19 is the most detailed. He will be betrayed, condemned by the Jews, and tortured by the Gentiles. (a) All three accounts predict Jesus' death, yet each also includes His resurrection on the third day—the most significant element (b) because it points to victory in the face of despair, death, and defeat. The disciples seem to miss this point entirely.

12. (a) Each of these passages indicate the disciples were afraid, grieved, and almost in shock. They didn't seem to understand anything Jesus was saying. They refused to accept the possibility of His death. Instead, they wanted Jesus to meet their expectations. (b) James and John may have changed the subject to avoid facing the fact that Jesus was truly the Suffering Servant rather than a powerful conquering King. (c) Their primary concern seems to be their own destiny, position, honor, and reputation.

13. As background, you might note that crowds followed Jesus to Jerusalem. Many in the crowd were probably pilgrims going to Jerusalem for Passover. A group of women traveled with Jesus and the disciples to care for practical needs along the way. One of these was Salome, the sister of Mary, the mother of Jesus. Salome was Zebedee's wife, mother of James and John. (These deductions concerning Salome result from a comparative study of Matthew 27:56; Mark 15:40–41; and John

19:25.) Matthew indicates Salome made the request in verse 21. Mark indicates James and John made the request for positions of supremacy. We can easily see that all three are interested in Jesus' response.

(a) Jesus seems to understand their confused and troubled state of mind. He doesn't scold or condemn, but once again He gently teaches them that they must share His suffering if they would share His glory. "To drink the cup" was an Old Testament symbol for suffering under the judgment of God. Jesus would "drink the cup" in His sacrificial death on the cross, where He took the judgment for our sins upon Himself.

(b) Jesus predicts that those who follow Him will suffer persecution as He did. Specifically, James was the first apostle to meet a martyr's death (Acts 12:2), and John was exiled for his faith (Revelation 1:9).

(c) Jesus is always the obedient servant of the Father as He relinquishes His position, His rights, His power. He models the humble servant until that time when God will exalt Him.

14. Power, position, prestige, fame and fortune, acclaim, attention, appreciation are highly valued by the world's standards. Jesus inverts human standards of greatness and teaches that greatness lies in ministry—in self-giving and self-spending. Ask group members to share summaries they have written.

Day 5 • Matthew 20:29–34; Mark 10:46–52; Luke 18:35–43

15. The blind men, told by the crowd that Jesus was going by, identify Him as the Messiah, calling Him "Lord, Son of David." They couldn't see the miracles He had performed, yet they believed.

16. (a) Those leading the procession scolded the blind men and told them to stop their shouting. Perhaps Jesus was teaching as they walked along, and they resented the interruption. (b) Jesus, however, stopped and called them. Jesus encourages them to express their need, heals them, and acknowledges their faith. Matthew stresses Jesus' compassion and loving touch. On His way to give His life He continues to serve the needs of others.

17. Encourage but don't force members to share answers. Assure one another that Jesus is interested in every aspect of our lives, but that His primary objective for us is that we learn to trust and follow Him.

18. Permit group members to share special insights, reaffirmed convictions, and unanswered questions.

Notes

The Disciples Learn to Talk about the Faith

Matthew 21–22

Preparing for the Session

Central Focus

The Large Catechism says, "The first things that issue and emerge from the heart are words" (LC I 50). Therefore, what is more natural for us disciples than talking about the Lord, the object of our faith? This lesson examines the words that Jesus spoke in His controversy with the religious leadership of Israel, words that teach us how to talk about our Lord and His salvation.

Objectives

That the participant, as a child of God and with the Holy Spirit's help, will be led to

1. talk about Jesus in everyday conversation;
2. understand that good works grow out of true faith;
3. produce good works through conversation;
4. center words of witness on faith in Jesus Christ.

For the Small-Group Leader

Many important things can be happening in the LifeLight discussion groups. The most basic of these activities, of course, is meeting with the living Christ through the Scriptures. Through your study of God's Word the Spirit will build you up in an awareness of God's will, in faith and trust in Him, and in love for Him.

As this occurs, love for one another as brothers and sisters in the Lord will also grow among you. This love will express itself in caring about and for one another. And this, in turn, will lead you to a deeper common concern for the Lord's kingdom. This concern will surely be expressed in prayer. As the group discussion leader, you will also want to be a prayer leader, one who fosters prayer in your group. Prayer will probably suggest itself at obvious points, such as at the beginning and end of the discussion session. But there will also be other points when prayer will seem the obvious thing to do, perhaps at discussion points which have been particularly helpful, moving, or enlightening.

These prayers need not be long or elaborate—in fact, they should not be. Prayers of only a few short sentences will accomplish the task. Nor does one person (probably yourself) need always to be the prayer leader. Rather, this joyful duty can be passed around among volunteers. This will bring variety and fullness to your group prayers.

Small-Group Discussion Helps

Day 1 • Matthew 21:1–11

1. Jesus' ride was a deliberate symbolic act to fulfill prophecy concerning the Messiah. A colt never before ridden was used for sacred purposes. The donkey was symbolic of humility and peace. Kings rode a donkey to demonstrate that they came in peace—in contrast to horses used in war. Jesus chose the donkey to claim publicly He was the chosen Son of David of whom the prophets spoke in Zechariah 9:9–10. (Jesus rode the colt with the mother donkey following. Matthew is the only Gospel writer to mention two animals.) Jesus came to Jerusalem to die in meekness, dependent on the power of God the Father, with no trappings, no weapons, except His Word.

2. Spreading cloaks on the road was an act of royal homage. Branches were used in victory celebrations. Only John identifies these as palm branches. John sees the multitude of the redeemed in heaven celebrating with palm branches in their hands. Later, after the resurrection, the disciples would understand that Jesus was indeed their victorious King over sin and death (John 12:16).

3. (a) Jesus was the King who could save His people from the distress of sin and death, the Messiah promised by God through David's line. (b) Jesus came

in God's name; He was the Lord's Anointed. He came with God's authority to defeat the enemies of sin, Satan, and death through His perfect life, death, and resurrection—all on our behalf. (c) The angels sang God's praise at Jesus' birth, and all in heaven praise Him eternally.

4. These descriptions or titles for Jesus are stated or implied in Matthew 21:1–11. Ask volunteers to share which are most meaningful to them and why. Emphasize that Jesus came in fulfillment of God's promises to defeat death, to cancel sin, and to bring peace to the hearts of the faithful.

Day 2 • Matthew 21:12–22

5. Jesus echoes the words of Isaiah and Jeremiah. He condemns those who take advantage of the poor, the lowly, the Gentiles, and also those authorities who allow these things to happen.

God's temple was meant to be a house of prayer for all people. The area outside the temple proper included the large outer court of the Gentiles. It covered several acres and was intended as a place for all to worship God at the temple. However, the Jews had allowed the court of the Gentiles to become a noisy, smelly marketplace.

Pilgrims to the Passover needed animals that met ritual requirements for sacrifice. They needed their money changed into local currency for paying the temple tax. The examiners of sacrificial animals were corrupt, turning down animals not purchased at the temple.

Doves sold at the temple cost 20 times more than those sold elsewhere. Money changers added surcharges up to a fourth of the actual tax or equal to two days' wages. In addition, the stalls were the personal property of the high priest and his family.

The Jewish leaders were allowing the temple area to be misused and were interfering with God's intentions for the Gentiles. They had robbed the temple of its sanctity and were taking financial advantage of the people. They had externalized and commercialized worship, all the while hiding behind a religious facade and plotting Jesus' death.

6. While priests and Levites had to be able-bodied according to the Law of Moses, nothing prohibited worshipers with disabilities from approaching God in worship (Leviticus 21:16–23). Jesus healed the hurting, while the religious leaders rejected them. The chief priests and teachers of the law were indignant and critical when the children praised the Lord. They wanted Jesus to silence the children. Their outrage led them to plot Jesus' death! But Jesus quotes the psalm that says God appoints and evokes the praise of little children to silence the enemies arrayed against Him. God deliberately chooses the weak and lowly to shame those who consider themselves so wise!

7. (a) Normally a fig tree in full leaf would be heavy with ripe fruit. Jesus could expect fruit on a tree with leaves. This fig tree is deceptive because its leaves are all out early. But it only *looks* ready. (b) **Challenge question.** The tree is a symbol of Israel's moral and religious character. Israel professes to believe in God and to be waiting for the Messiah. Yet Israel refuses to bring forth the fruit of repentance and receive Jesus. Instead, Israel's leaders are ready to kill Him. Jesus has patiently repeated His call to repentance (Luke 13:5–9) during the three years of His ministry. Now time is running out. Cursing the fig tree shows God's judgment operative through the Messiah. Blasting the fig tree symbolizes Jesus' judgment on the Jews' hollow piety that produces no fruit of repentance and faith.

8. (a) Jesus contrasts the lack of faith in Israel with the powerful faith of those who do believe. Jesus seems to be saying: Nothing is impossible for those who in faith tap God's power through prayer. This does not mean, however, that God answers every prayer of ours in the way that we expect. (b) Prayer must be in accord with God's will (Mark 14:36; 1 John 5:14). And God may well say no to what we ask when a yes would harm us (2 Corinthians 12:7–9). We certainly should not conclude that our faith is weak or displeasing to God if He does not immediately grant our every request. Jesus is here speaking figuratively and not literally.

Day 3 • Matthew 21:23–22:14

9. Holy Week began with the triumphal entry into

Jerusalem on Sunday. The next day Jesus drove out the merchants and money changers from the temple, heightening the confrontation with the chief priests and elders. On Tuesday the controversy continued. By His actions on Monday, Jesus defied the authority of the Jewish leaders. Now, when the leaders question Jesus' authority, He refuses to answer because they cannot answer His question, admitting their inability to discern what is from God and what is not. Their failure disqualifies them as teachers and leaders, and therefore removes their right to question Jesus. If they will not acknowledge that John was sent by God to call them to repentance and to offer them forgiveness, then Jesus cannot tell them of His authority—for it is revealed in His ministry and in His mercy to those who feel their need of mercy. These men refuse to admit their need.

10. (a) The parable of the two sons illustrates the contrast in reactions to John's message. The father represents God the Father. The son who first refused but then obeyed represents the tax collectors and prostitutes who repented at John's call and returned to God. The son who agreed but then refused to go represents those Jews who politely professed obedience but refused to repent, preferring to argue about authority! Jesus accuses them of refusing John's teaching and his baptism of repentance and Jesus' teachings and works.

(b) Like the son who first agreed but then did not go, we may say yes to God with our lips but then not carry through in our obedience to Him (as when we agree in a confirmation vow to be faithful to death but then give in to temptation). Like the son who refused but later went, we may defy God and then later repent.

11. The religious leaders refused to listen to John and to acknowledge that the only way to righteousness is through repentance and faith in Jesus, who gives us righteousness through His life, death, and resurrection (Philippians 3:9).

Their self-righteous attitude clarifies the terrible dangers in never being willing to admit we are wrong and in need of His mercy and help. Hopefully, the atmosphere you are building in your group encourages candor, honesty, support, and love so that repentance and faith may grow.

12. In the parable of the two sons the emphasis was on what happened in the past. In the parable of the tenants the emphasis is on the present and future. Jesus is aware of death plots against Him and warns of the serious consequences.

(a) The landowner represents God; the vineyard represents the nation of Israel (Isaiah 5:1–7), His people, the object of His love and care; the tenant farmers are the religious leaders; the landowner's servants are the Old Testament prophets; the son is Jesus; and the other tenants are the Gentiles (Acts 13:46).

(b) In this parable Jesus clearly claims to be God's Son. Instead of accepting the Son and turning to Him in obedience and faith, the wicked tenants have rejected Him and plan to kill Him. The warning is clear: those who reject Jesus the Messiah will be doomed (Isaiah 8:14 and Luke 2:34).

13. Here are two parables in one: the parable of the wedding banquet (vv. 1–10) and the parable of the guest with no wedding garment (vv. 11–14). The first parable pictures God's rejection of Israel; the second pictures God's response to the individual.

The king represents God; the servants are the prophets of the past and the apostles of the future; the wedding banquet is the kingdom of heaven (Revelation 19:1, 7); the invited guests who refused the invitation are those Jews who refused to receive Jesus as the Messiah; the people from the street corners are the Gentiles; the wedding garment is the righteousness God graciously provides for those who respond to His invitation; and the outer darkness is the state of final damnation and punishment (Revelation 20:14; 21:8).

According to Jewish custom, invitations were sent far in advance. Then, when all was prepared, the guests were summoned. Apparently the invitations had been accepted. But when the summons came, some invited guests ignored it or made light of it—that's why the refusal was such an insult. The parable pictures the open opposition to God's representatives, such as John the Baptist.

14. Dressed in our own garments of self-righteousness we are pitiful, filthy, and ragged. But dressed in the

clothes God provides we appear in clean, shining bridal garb, clothed in Christ's righteousness. This is the message of the second parable (vv. 11–14). Without the clothes Christ gives, we miss the joy of the wedding feast. The guest insisting on wearing his or her own soiled self-righteousness despises the grace of the king and invites judgment. When judgment comes, the pain is the pain of regret (gnashing of teeth) for the joy that was lost.

Day 4 • Matthew 22:15–40

15. So long as secular governments stay within the realm God has assigned to them (providing protection and fostering the welfare of citizens in regard to this world) and do not encroach upon areas that God has reserved for Himself (worship of God, trust in Him for salvation from sin, and obedience to His laws), there will be no conflict between secular government and God's kingdom. God's people will then gladly obey and cheerfully support secular government, giving this government the honor God Himself gives it. But whenever secular governments call upon citizens to give to them the worship and honor we can only give to God, or command us to act contrary to God's holy Law, we must obey God, even if this means disobeying civil authorities. In the apostolic era, Peter refused to cease proclaiming Christ, and Christians refused to worship the Roman emperor as a god. In both past and present times, many other Christians have courageously endured hardship, torture, and death rather than compromise faith in Christ and obedience to Him.

16. Matthew considers this question a further test of Jesus. Mark pictures the teacher of the law as an earnest individual, "not far from the kingdom of God." The question is straightforward and simple. It poses no hypothetical situation. It was not out of the ordinary since Jewish rabbis often tried to distinguish between "heavy" and "light" commands in the Law. Thus Jesus' answer might not appear as controversial.

(a) Jesus quoted from Deuteronomy 6:5 and Leviticus 19:18. The common command is to love. Love—for God and for others—is the overriding will of God.

(b) Jesus shows the unbroken unity between love for God and love for others. Out of love for the Father, Jesus was perfectly obedient to the Father's will. Out of love for sinners, Jesus sacrificed Himself in obedience to the Father. Jesus loved God the Father; Jesus loved sinners. He models the love the Father wills.

(c) When we measure our love for God and one another against the demands of the Law, we see our sin. Such total, unselfish love is impossible for sinners.

(d) Assure one another that Scripture also includes Gospel—the Good News that God is ready to forgive our lovelessness and daily energize us with His Spirit.

Day 5 • Matthew 22:41–46

17. In this exchange with the Pharisees Jesus makes His greatest claim. Jesus shows, by quoting David's psalm, that the descendant (Lord) David refers to is more than a human descendant. He is divine. Jesus Himself is this divine descendant. Jesus invites the Pharisees to confess Him as the promised Messiah. Jesus calls them to repentance and faith. They, however, want a human conqueror like David, an earthly son of David who will be a great and powerful deliverer from Roman rule, one who will make them and their nation great.

18. The Pharisees dared not reply for fear that, in their own minds, they would be committing blasphemy. Only true repentance and the indwelling Spirit could lead them to acknowledge Jesus as Son of God and Messiah. To answer Jesus' question they must admit the Messiah was also the divine Son of God. This they would not do.

19. Perhaps the Pharisees retreated in silence, confident that now they had, in Jesus' declaration, the evidence they needed to accuse Him of blasphemy. They surely understood what He meant, for they remembered what He said and used it against Him later.

20. Encourage group members to share new insights, strengthened convictions, and remaining questions.

Small-Group Leaders Session 6 — Matthew Part 2

Jesus Condemns His Unrepentant Opponents

Matthew 23

Preparing for the Session

Central Focus

Appearances are deceiving. Without God's Word, we are not only deceived but are led into the woes of despair and the condemnation of hell. However, in God's Word we have an infallible basis for faith and life.

Objectives

That the participant, as a child of God and with the Holy Spirit's help, will be led to

1. appreciate as never before that "The LORD does not look at the things man looks at. Man looks at the outward appearance, but the LORD looks at the heart" (1 Samuel 16:7);
2. depend upon God and His revealed Word;
3. let words of woe and condemnation drive him or her to the Savior.

For the Small-Group Discussion Leader

You will need to be ready to provide some extra guidance as your group discusses the Scripture assigned for this week. Chapter 23 records Jesus' harshest and most thorough condemnation of the scribes and Pharisees who refused to repent and to believe the Gospel. Help your group avoid pitfalls.

It would be easy to point an accusing finger at the Pharisees and let it go at that. After all, Jesus Himself condemns them; why shouldn't we? Simply to do this and no more, however, would be an attempt to short-circuit the Spirit's use of Scripture. The Pharisees are long gone; their judgment is sealed. The question at hand is, What does this Scripture say to us?

We might be prone to find contemporary Pharisees and direct Jesus' condemnation toward them. About this we need to be extremely careful. Jesus can see into the heart; we cannot. We need to hear Jesus' warning: "Do not judge, or you too will be judged. For in the same way you judge others, you will be judged, and with the measure you use, it will be measured to you" (Matthew 7:1–2).

Or we might be prone to apply Jesus' hard words to ourselves. This is closer to the mark; like the Pharisees of old, we too need to hear the Law that condemns hypocrisy. We may discover the seeds of this sin in our own hearts. But applying the Law should be done carefully and in the proper measure. Remember the Pharisees addressed in this chapter were unrepentant; to those who do repent Jesus offers the sweet comfort of forgiveness and peace. When the Law has done its work within us, it is then time to hear the Gospel, to receive the Lord's forgiveness, and to rejoice in our restoration. Encourage one another to permit the Gospel to have the last word.

Small-Group Discussion Helps

Day 1 • Matthew 23:1–12

1. Jesus condemns the Pharisees' hypocrisy, spiritual pride, egotism, and their tendency to show off for others. Their piety was aimed at men, not God—therefore it was false and empty.

2. (a) Hypocrites do not practice what they preach. (b) Encourage group members to be candid in their responses. Possible responses may include the following: I would feel insulted, embarrassed, angry, unjustly judged, misunderstood. (c) Possible responses may include the following: lash out, try to justify my actions, explain, take a long, hard look at my behavior.

3. (a) The burden the Pharisees laid on people's backs was the system of rules and regulations they insisted must be kept in order to enter the Kingdom. (b) These rules became a heavy burden, especially for those who-

had to work for a living. Worse yet was the fact that the burden of trying to keep the Law was an impossible task. (c) The Law is to show us our sin and our need for the Savior. (d) The Pharisees did nothing to help the people with their burden of keeping the Law or with the guilt of failure to keep it. (e) In contrast Jesus came to minister in mercy, bear people's burdens, fulfill the Law for them, and give rest to those who are heavy laden (11:28–30).

4. (a) The teachers of the law and the Pharisees behaved like hypocrites when they wore oversized phylacteries and tassels, sought seats of honor, and desired prestigious titles. (b) In contrast Jesus was gentle and humble and didn't draw attention to Himself.

5. **Challenge question.** (a) The original purpose of the phylacteries was to help Israel remember, study, cherish, and share the Law of the Lord so they would continue to love and serve God. (b) Likewise the tassels were to remind them to follow and obey God, who saved them from the Egyptians. (c) The Pharisees used the phylacteries and fringes to advertise their own piety, focusing on themselves instead of God. (d) Hypocrites want to be noticed. They want to show off their piety. (e) The scribes and Pharisees sought after the respect, power, and praise these titles carry.

6. Jesus emphasizes a leadership style characterized by humble service.

Day 2 • Matthew 23:13–22

7. Throughout His ministry Jesus showed His acceptance, love, mercy, pity, and compassion. He calmed fears, welcomed the lowly, affirmed their worth, sought out the lost, and emphasized by His example the importance of humility and trust. His tone of loving encouragement and support is clear. In contrast He condemns the Pharisees.

8. (a) By substituting their own ideas and rules, the Pharisees were shutting the door to the Kingdom in the faces of the people they influenced. By refusing to follow Jesus they influenced the people to reject Him. They had become a barrier rather than a guide to the Kingdom. (b) The Pharisees wanted converts to Judaism. They sought converts to earn merits. Some of their converts became fanatics about keeping the laws. They became as hypocritical and legalistic as the Pharisees. (c) The Pharisees were misleading the people with their frivolous teachings about oaths. They taught that certain oaths were more binding than others. They encouraged lying, evasion, and the manipulation of situations to suit themselves.

9. (a) The Pharisees were blind to their own error. More than anyone else in Israel, they influenced the people. (b) The teachings of the Pharisees must have burdened, confused, frustrated, and discouraged the people by setting up impossible standards of conduct. What is worse, the Pharisees led the people to trust in themselves instead of God's mercy—with disastrous results. Their teachings interfered with the call of Jesus to the kingdom of God.

Day 3 • Matthew 23:23–28

10. (a) Jesus supports the tithe of produce. These Pharisees were concerned with the trifles of the law, tithing the tiny herb plants of the kitchen garden while at the same time neglecting what really mattered. Jesus condemns their lack of justice, mercy, and faithfulness. The Pharisees had refused to yield their hearts to Him. (b) Jesus uses the illustration of straining a gnat and swallowing a camel to show that the Pharisees have their priorities confused. In order to avoid the risk of drinking anything unclean, such as a tiny gnat, the Pharisees strained their wine through gauze. Yet Jesus pictures them as cheerfully swallowing a camel! They toyed with trifles while neglecting to forgive others, behave honestly, care for aged parents, or repent and believe in Jesus.

11. (a) The Pharisees appear to be clean—deeply religious, zealous, and righteous. (b) Jesus pictures the Pharisees as clean on the outside but filthy on the inside. Their hearts are corrupt, filled with greed and self-indulgence.

12. (a) Jesus compares the Pharisees to these whitewashed tombs that looked clean and beautiful on the outside, but were full of death and decay within. (b) Jesus is more concerned about the condition of our hearts than about our external appearance.

Matthew Part 2 — Small-Group Leaders Session 6

Day 4 • Matthew 23:29–36

13. (a) The Pharisees pretended to be innocent of rejecting and killing the Old Testament prophets. But while they tried to disclaim their forefathers who shed the blood of the prophets, yet—because they refused to obey God's Word—the Pharisees shared their fathers' guilt. (b) While the Pharisees made a show of honoring the prophets by beautifying their tombs, their true attitude was shown in their attitude toward Jesus. Jesus predicts they would complete their forefathers' sin by putting Him to death. They would also persecute His disciples. (c) The Pharisees have refused for three years to repent and believe in Jesus as God's Messiah. Time has run out. Their hearts have not softened. Without repentance they face condemnation. Their hatred of Jesus will lead them to hell.

14. The Pharisees fulfill Jesus' predictions by arresting and imprisoning His disciples after murdering Stephen. (Note that among these Pharisees was Saul—soon to become Paul, a disciple of the same Jesus he joined in persecuting!)

15. Jesus uses an expression somewhat like our "from Genesis to Revelation." (Chronicles was the last book in the Old Testament according to the Hebrew arrangement.) Because of their stubborn refusal to accept the prophets and the Christ, the Pharisees can expect to be held responsible for their unbelief and condemned to hell. Such talk sounds unusually harsh coming from Jesus. Yet we know He does not want any person to be forever lost. This is a final attempt to alert the Pharisees to the seriousness of rejecting Him. Such an outburst should sober us also to the dangers of hypocrisy and self-idolatry.

Day 5 • Matthew 23:37–39

16. Jesus reveals the longing of His loving heart—to draw every person, including the Jews, to Himself. One almost detects a sob in these poignant words. Condemnation brings Him no pleasure; it hurts Him. Rejection hurts Jesus too. Yet He loved so much that He was willing to suffer rejection (and more) to save us all.

17. Jesus holds out the hope that at least some of the Jews will welcome and receive Him. In that hope, the Christian church today continues to offer the Gospel to all—Jews and Gentiles alike. Paul, a devout Pharisee, came to true faith after Jesus' ascension. Some Jews believed Paul's message. Salvation in the New Testament, like salvation in the Old Testament, comes to individuals as God's gift of grace received by faith and not on the basis of one's nationality.

18. Jesus appeals to us through the Gospel. His Word to us comes in many forms—in the context of worship and Bible study, in the Sacraments, in personal Bible reading and prayer, in the words of absolution, in the witness of other Christians. Wherever Jesus appeals to us to repent, be forgiven, trust, and follow Him, we listen and respond by the prompting of His Spirit. Our response is evident in how we arrange our priorities.

Help one another to see all of life from this perspective—as a time God gives each of us to hear Him calling, to yield our hearts to Him, and to learn to trust Him completely, until we are at last gathered close to His heart forever.

19. Invite participants to share an insight, a renewed conviction, a question.

Notes

Jesus Prepares His Disciples for the End Times

Matthew 24–25

Preparing for the Session

Central Focus

In the hymn "God of Grace and God of Glory," Harry Emerson Fosdick wrote words terribly true of our society: *Rich in things and poor in soul.* Jesus' prophecies about the end of the world teach us to be critical of contemporary society and help us ready our souls for His return.

Objectives

That the participant, as a child of God and with the help of the Holy Spirit, will be led to

1. value more highly the things of the soul;
2. develop a more biblical attitude toward time;
3. become more critically aware of our society;
4. lose self in service to Christ.

Small-Group Discussion Helps

Day 1 • Matthew 24:1–31

1. The disciples came from Galilee. They may not have visited Jerusalem often. Herod's temple was impressive, and they mentioned this to Jesus as they passed by. The massive white stones of the temple, some 40 feet long and weighing as much as 100 tons, were overlaid with gold. The huge temple, built on a hill, was a dazzling sight. Jesus predicts that the temple will be leveled—that not one stone will be left on another. Only a powerful, terrible force could do that. No wonder the disciples question Jesus further!

2. (a) The disciples asked Jesus, first, "When will the present age end?"; second, "What signs will signal your return?"; third, "What signs will signal the end of this age?" (b) Jesus describes the troubles the world will experience during this period: false prophets, wars, strife, trouble, distress, famines, and earthquakes. Jesus tells His disciples that He wants them to understand that these things must happen as part of the process of all history culminating in His return.

3. (a) Jesus predicts that Christians will be persecuted, martyred, scorned, and hated. They will be misled and deceived by false prophets. There will be internal dissension—hatred and a lack of love. Some will abandon their faith and shame Christ. They will be led into immorality.

(b) All of this is very discouraging to the church; yet we find hope and promise here in verses 13–14. God is at work. Faith will endure. The Gospel will reach every nation before the end comes! With courage and patience the faithful believe and live! (Hebrews 10:32–39).

Discuss how Jesus' predictions are being fulfilled today—both inside and outside the church. Point out how discouragement becomes Satan's mighty tool to pry us away from Jesus. Reemphasize faith as gift.

4. The "abomination that causes desolation" refers to the detestable thing causing desolation in the Holy Place. Antiochus Epiphanes sacrificed a pig on the altar in 168 B.C., in fulfillment of Daniel's prophecy. Around A.D. 37–41, the Roman emperor Caligula attempted to set up his own statue for worship in the temple. Pagan armies desecrated the temple during the Roman siege.

(a) Jesus told His followers to flee Jerusalem immediately. If time will allow, share that some Christians followed the Lord's directions and fled to the mountain city of Pella, where they were safe. Others sought protection inside the walls of Jerusalem, where they suffered terrible famine. Josephus, Jewish historian and eyewitness, described the horrible suffering (v. 21) of the Jews at the hands of the Roman army.

(b) Jesus is concerned for women and children who would find travel difficult and strenuous. Traveling in winter when heavy rains caused flooding or on the Sabbath when travel was restricted would cause problems. Jesus is concerned about this. He assures the disciples that God will shorten the suffering for His people.

5. Encourage participants to share their paraphrases with the group. Jesus warns us ahead of time to beware of anyone who pretends to know when and where He will appear. Jesus' coming will be sudden and unexpected. But when He does come it will be obvious to everyone. (The proverb in verse 28 means the coming of Christ will be as obvious as the gathering of vultures around a carcass.)

6. Encourage everyone to share what Jesus seems to be saying to each of them. Remind one another that although the waiting period seems long, the Day of the LORD will surely come. God's judgment will fall, and unbelievers will mourn. Jesus will come in glory and gather His own to Himself. We can be sure of this. No matter what happens, we know God is in control, moving everything toward this final moment. We are secure, knowing our Lord has taken care to show us the signs of His coming and the meaning of a seemingly chaotic world. We find comfort in dark days, sensing the nearness of His return and the promise of being with Him. We are strengthened to endure until the ultimate triumph of Jesus, our King. Anticipation displaces dread; hope—discouragement; courage—fear; joy—sorrow.

Day 2 • Matthew 24:32–51

7. When the fig tree begins to leaf we know summer is near. So also when we see the signs Jesus has predicted earlier in chapter 24, we know the Day of the LORD is drawing near. Just as we can wait with patience, aware of the signs of the coming seasons, so also we can wait for Jesus to come, confident God is in charge. We can count on Jesus' sure, eternal Word.

8. Just as in the days of Noah people were preoccupied with the things and affairs of this life and were therefore unprepared for the suddenness of the flood, so also the sudden, unpredictable coming of Jesus will catch many unbelievers unprepared. The days in both cases are deceptively normal! Scoffers follow their own evil desires. Workers go about their daily tasks. Yet the time of separation comes. Jesus gathers up His own.

9. How many in your group have taken security measures in their homes? Dead bolts, bars on windows, alarm systems, and watchdogs are common precautions against burglary, especially in urban areas. It takes time, money, and planning to be prepared against thieves. Vigilance is necessary if the unexpected intruder is to be stopped. So also the Christian must keep watch and be ready for the unexpected coming of the Lord. (The difference is that we are not afraid of what we may lose!)

10. (a) Jesus compares His disciples to trusted servants who are given remarkable responsibilities. The master provides, and the servants manage the resources. They have the power and authority to feed the entire household. These servants are blessed when the master returns and finds them faithfully at work. So also, we are to feed one another with the Word of life, faithfully managing the resources of the Gospel.

(b) Wicked servants grow tired of waiting. They live in the delusion that there is plenty of time before the master returns. They victimize their fellow servants. They fail to use what they've been given for the good of others. They waste themselves in self-indulgence.

Day 3 • Matthew 25:1–13

11. The foolish girls seem no different from the wise—except that the foolish girls were not fully prepared to meet the bridegroom. They hadn't sufficient oil to keep their lamps lit. The wise bridesmaids, however, were responsible and had prepared well.

12. Encourage participants to share answers. Possible responses may include the delay made them careless; they had become complacent; they lost interest after a while; they became self-indulgent; they thought there was plenty of time for a nap.

13. (a) Encourage sharing. Possible responses may include embarrassed, disappointed, panicked, chagrined, worried, or concerned.

(b) Apparently they falsely assumed they could rely on

the others to help them out. They also assumed they could change the bridegroom's mind and make him open the door through pleading (and perhaps tears). Possibly they didn't really believe he would shut them out of the celebration!

(c) Allow for personal responses and reasons. Obviously, if the oil was shared no one would make it to the celebration; the light would go out before all of them got there. The wise girls offer good advice. Each individual must be sufficiently supplied; all that is needed seems readily available.

(d) Let participants share. The oil of the parable corresponds to faith given to us as the Spirit touches our hearts with His Word—the spoken Word, the Word we read, and the visible Word of Baptism and the Lord's Supper. How important—eternally so!—that we put ourselves in a position where the Holy Spirit can minister to us, stirring up faith through His Word.

14. According to verse 11 the girls were frantic to get in. They wanted to be included in the celebration. Perhaps they accepted rejection with the same weeping and gnashing of teeth as the others who only appeared to belong to Jesus (Matthew 8:12; 22:13; 24:51).

Day 4 • Matthew 25:14–30

15. **Challenge question.** (a–f) The man going on a journey represents Jesus, about to leave His disciples. The property (or talents) of the master represents the Lord's "goods," or the truth of the Gospel. This truth, formerly hidden, has been revealed in Jesus for all the world to know and includes God's purpose and plan in the incarnation of His Son, His death and resurrection, and God's call to both Jew and Gentile to enter His kingdom by faith. (See 1 Corinthians 4:1–2 and Matthew 13:52.) In the parable the master's property is in the form of talents (weight in coinage). (*Talent* here does not mean a skill or ability.) The man's servants represent all Christians who have been given the grace of God in the Gospel. The period of absence is the time from Jesus' ascension until His return. The man's return is Christ's Second Coming. The settling of accounts is the final judgment.

16. (a) Knowledge, insight, and understanding of the Gospel are given to each Christian—but in the measure decided upon by the Master. The servant's responsibility is to be faithful in using what he or she has been given—to allow it to grow, develop, and mature; to share it, sow it till it multiplies and spreads; to translate it into loving service for the good of others. (This is where the use of God-given talents—in the narrower sense—fits in.)

The five-talent servant and the two-talent servant were faithful. They took risks to grow, to share, to serve. They put what they had been given to work. The one-talent servant took no risks. He did no work—no growing, sharing, or serving. He played it safe. (Burying a treasure in those days was the best way to ensure its safety.) Jesus teaches His disciples that He has entrusted them (and us) with the Gospel, and He looks for faithful service from those who work to share it during the time of waiting until His return.

(b) The master graciously gives the same reward to each of the faithful servants. The master measures by faithfulness. Both faithful servants share the master's happiness, just as faithful stewards of the Gospel receive eternal life by God's grace.

17. (a) The one-talent servant says in effect, "If you hadn't been hard and made me afraid, I could have done more. This is what you get for expecting so much." He somehow feels justified in handing back to his master the "property" exactly as it was. He seems resentful. He failed to trust his master's love.

(b) He was wicked in his selfishness. No one else benefited from the proper use of the master's treasure. When we bury the Gospel instead of investing it through a life of witness, love, and service, we are guilty of wasting opportunities to grow, share, and serve—to bless others. The servant was lazy. He didn't even bother to take advantage of "bank interest" (v. 27). He avoided any responsibility. Those who know the truth have the responsibility to share the truth.

18. (a) The servant is worthless because he has not allowed the treasure to multiply. He has been faithless. He has failed to trust the master's grace and power to bless his efforts with success.

Jesus chose to send the Good News to the whole world on the lips and in the hands of His disciples. This was His plan. He puts us in charge. Though it looks like a formidable task, He asks us to trust Him, to take risks, to spend our time and energies faithfully in His service. What's more, He blesses it with success by the power of His Spirit!

(b) Jesus promises that the treasure is His. We do not preach ourselves, but Christ. Jesus promises He will return and settle accounts. All time moves toward that culminating point. Therefore there is purpose in our service. Jesus promises that those who are faithful will share His joy.

Day 5 • Matthew 25:31–46

19. (a) The Judge is the Shepherd who gave His life for the sheep. He separates the sheep (the believers) from the goats (the unbelievers) on the basis of their faith. (b) It is significant that the separation takes place before any mention of deeds. Jesus has said, "He who is not with Me is against Me" (12:30). The deeds of mercy (35–36) express the fact that the believers are with Jesus. Be sure these points are clear in your discussion, otherwise the text will seem to promote salvation based on human works, good deeds, rather than on God's grace. It's worth noting also that our Lord calls eternal life an "inheritance" (v. 34)—an unearned gift.

20. (a) The sheep follow the Shepherd. Just as Jesus was compassionate and merciful as He ministered, so also His sheep show mercy in acts of kindness, concern, love, and care. (b) The merciful find God's mercy in the judgment. The Judge doesn't even mention their failures!

21. The unmerciful are committed to the unmerciful enemy of God—Satan and his angels. They share their doom.

22. Share personal responses. When we recognize Christ within our brothers and sisters we are moved to respond to them in love, reflecting the compassion Jesus Himself has shown. Yet our response to others is not disguised self-interest (v. 44); it arises from genuine empathy and concern.

23. Encourage participants to share an insight, conviction, or question.

Notes

Jesus Redeems Disciples in the Crisis of the Cross

Matthew 26–27

Preparing for the Session

Central Focus

Judas, Peter, and Jesus. One didn't survive. One did, only by forgiving grace. And one died and rose to give us His Holy Spirit that we might know and love Him more and more. The study of these three can equip our faith to withstand our times of crisis.

Objectives

That the participant, as a child of God and with the Holy Spirit's help, will be led to

1. appreciate the real life crises of Judas, Peter, and Jesus;

2. make zealous use of the calm times in life, "before the days of trouble come" (Ecclesiastes 12:1);

3. make the death of Christ the constant occupation of a willing spirit, in prayer, in worship, in remembrance, and in confident hope.

For the Small-Group Leader

In this week's Scripture we arrive at the very heart of the mystery of God's love for us as He gives His one and only Son into death on the cross for us. As you discuss Scripture this week, share with your group your appreciation and praise as you consider Jesus' sacrifice and the Father's love in giving us this most wonderful gift of salvation. Let your group sense your own wonder and awe at God's love for us. Let your feelings about what God has done for you be evident; wear your heart on your sleeve in this week's session.

Small-Group Discussion Helps

Day 1 • Matthew 26:1–16 and John 12:1–11

1. (a) Jesus knows His death is fast approaching (26:2, 12). He has deliberately come to Jerusalem, confronted His enemies, and accepted the way of the cross.

(b) The chief priests and elders plot to kill Jesus and bribe Judas to betray Him. It was not their plan to kill Jesus during Passover (v. 5); nevertheless, God had His way (Acts 4:23–28 and Romans 8:32).

(c) The woman in verse 7 is Mary of Bethany (John 12:1–3). (This incident, though similar, is not the same as the one recorded in Luke 7:36–50.) Mary's love is a striking contrast to the plotting of the religious leaders and the cruel betrayal of Judas. Anointing the head was a common custom at feasts. Here Mary shows her utterly humble devotion to Jesus by anointing His feet. She spends her gift lavishly. Matthew estimates the value of the fragrant oil as equal to a year's wages! Most important is the fact that Mary believed Jesus' predictions about His coming death. She took His word seriously and prepared Him for death by comforting His heart with her love (vv. 10–13).

(d) The disciples show no reaction to Jesus' prediction of His death. They are critical of Mary's action, squabble and nitpick, and miss the point.

(e) John indicates it is Judas who objects the strongest. He kept the money bag in which were kept offerings for the poor. Judas had often dipped into the bag. Did he resent his own potential financial losses? Perhaps he resented his shaken hopes and fallen dreams. Perhaps Judas followed Jesus with the hope of sharing power, prestige, and privilege in His kingdom. Now he senses that a cross lies ahead for Jesus instead of a crown. In any case, he plotted to betray the Lord.

Perhaps Judas resented Jesus' death, while Jesus accepted it, the chief priests plotted it, Mary prepared for it, and the disciples ignored it.

2. Jesus honors Mary's loving act when He calls it beautiful. Help group members identify beautiful, loving actions in one another, such as encouraging rather than criticizing, patiently shouldering someone else's responsibility without complaint, cleaning up after a sick child, being patient with an elderly relative, forgiving … again and again, loving someone who cannot return love.

Day 2 • Matthew 26:17–46

3. Jesus and the disciples would celebrate the Passover according to God's commands given to Moses and Aaron in Egypt. The first day of the feast was a day of preparation. The meal was eaten that evening and a week-long festival began, celebrating God's deliverance of His people from bondage and death in Egypt.

In the first Passover a lamb was sacrificed; the blood of the lamb marked the families of God; punishment and death did not strike those protected by the blood of the lamb. Jesus is God's new Passover Lamb (1 Corinthians 5:7), without spot or defect, put to death to bring to life those marked with His blood. Because of His sacrifice, all who believe in Him celebrate their deliverance from sin, death, and Satan's power.

4. The disciples asked about the betrayer's identity (v. 22; John 13:21–25). Even guilty Judas feigns ignorance (v. 25). Judas' betrayal is heightened by the fact that he has dipped bread together with Jesus into a common bowl at supper. It was a common custom to dip bread in sauce at the table signifying "I am your friend. I will not hurt you."

Jesus may have been trying even at this late hour to lead Judas to repentance and faith. The Lord, in love, did not want to lose Judas. But Judas resists Jesus' love. Revealed as betrayer, Judas must now act quickly. Jesus' enemies are forced to arrest and kill Him at the Passover feast. Although that was not their original intent (26:5), apparently it was Jesus' intent. He becomes God's Passover Lamb.

5. (a) Jesus' blood seals God's new covenant (agreement) with sinners. Because Jesus shed His blood and paid for our sins, God promises we can come to Him, receive forgiveness, faith and hope, and the wonderful promise of eternal life. We are declared righteous by God through faith in Jesus. We trust in God's forgiveness, assured that He forgets the wrongs we've done!

(b) Encourage participants to share what they've written in response to this question.

6. (a) Jesus quoted Zechariah (13:7–9), who pictures the Good Shepherd struck by God's justice. The immediate effect is the dispersal, trial, and sifting of the flock, who are eventually restored as a trusting people. For the moment, however, the disciples fail Jesus miserably. Peter boasts the strongest devotion and produces the most flagrant denial. The disciples fall asleep, fail to be supportive, desert Jesus, and run away.

(b) Jesus knows the disciples will fail Him; yet He promises to be with them, to meet them in Galilee where, on the mount of His ascension and in the power of His resurrection, He will give them the authority to spread the Good News (28:7, 10, 16–20). Victory will come. Fellowship will be restored. There is encouragement here for us, too, as we daily fail Jesus. He promises that our falling away can be forgiven—that He will not abandon us, but rather will restore us to Himself.

7. (a) Late at night, after the Passover meal and a long conversation with His disciples (John 13–17) Jesus leads the way to Gethsemane, an olive garden east of Jerusalem. It is a private place where they can be alone for a while. Here Jesus faces the intense loneliness that comes from being separated from God the Father on account of sin. Jesus had never experienced the disapproval of His Father because of sin. Now He anticipates the agony of bearing the burden of the whole world's sin (2 Corinthians 5:21) and drinking the cup of the Father's wrath (Psalm 75:8)! What's more, He agonizes in the temptation to avoid it all!

(b) Through fellowship with His Father in prayer Jesus accepts God's answer that He alone must drink the cup of judgment on sin (Hebrews 5:7–9; 12:2). He has been strengthened, knowing His will is aligned with His Father's will (John 4:34; 6:38). Jesus has received the encouragement He sought and is ready to face the cross.

Day 3 • Matthew 26:47–75

8. (a) In calling Judas "Friend," Jesus may have been calling him to correction and repentance, assuring him that He would be there for him once Judas realized his sin. God uses the sin of man to carry out His purposes, but that does not excuse Judas (Romans 3:5–8). If only he had trusted Jesus to love and forgive him! Scripture assures us that Jesus reconciles us to God through His death.

(b) Encourage group members to share their answers here. Remind one another that although we fail and betray our Lord by sinning against Him every day, still He calls us to repentance, assures us of His constant love, and forgives us fully and freely. Daily He leads us in obedience by the power of the Holy Spirit. He has proved to be our dearest friend by laying down His life for us. Therefore we need never despair over sin as Judas did, but rather we live close to Him in His Word every day.

9. Jesus rebukes Peter when he draws a sword in His defense. Jesus reminds him that He has thousands of angels at His disposal who would come to His aid if He wished to escape. Jesus makes it plain that He is allowing His arrest in fulfillment of messianic prophecies (Zechariah 13:7 and Isaiah 53).

10. Jesus refuses to respond to the false evidence offered against Him (Isaiah 53:7), but when the high priest charged Jesus under oath (v. 63) He was legally obliged to reply. It was for this statement (v. 64) that Jesus was accused of blasphemy. The authorities considered Jesus' claim to be the Messiah an affront to the majesty and authority of God. Jesus was executed because He claimed to be God. When Caiaphas tore his clothing it was a sign of great grief and shock, albeit not sincere. It became a judicial act—a statement that Jesus was guilty.

11. (a) Peter was self-assured. He trusted his own ability to remain steadfast; he even boasted of his own superiority. He underestimated the cost of being loyal to Jesus. He overestimated his own power; he couldn't even stay awake when Jesus asked. He seems unaware of the temptations that surround him. He impulsively tries to take charge, swinging a sword, perhaps in an attempt to make up for his earlier foolishness. Although he flees with the others, he follows Jesus and risks recognition himself. When confronted, Peter denies Jesus with swearing and curses. And for all this he suffers an intense sorrow.

(b) Judas despaired of Jesus' love (27:1–5); Peter did not. Peter learned of his own helplessness against sin. He surely learned to trust himself less and Jesus more. Both Judas and Peter learned they could never undo what they had done. But it was Peter who learned that Jesus could forgive him for what he had done and that He could still use him in sharing the Good News of His mercy (John 21:15–19). Peter learned to trust Jesus' word.

Day 4 • Matthew 27:1–31

12. (a) Things hadn't worked out as Judas expected. When Jesus was condemned, Judas could see the painful consequences of his sin. Perhaps Judas expected to reverse the consequences of his betrayal by confessing to the high priest and returning the bribe, thus saving himself. But Judas confessed to the wrong person. The high priest was not interested in mercy. In self-centered sorrow, Judas despaired. His remorse led to his death. In contrast, Peter's sorrow over his sin (26:75) led to repentance and a change of heart. His was a God-centered sorrow over the wickedness of his sin. Peter did not despair. He waited for mercy (John 21:15–25).

(b) David trusted the mercy of God, His unfailing love, His great compassion. David believed that when he confessed his sin honestly to God, God would cleanse him from sin, blot out his iniquity, and renew him with His Spirit. Judas had witnessed Jesus' mercy, yet failed to trust His mercy, to accept it for himself personally.

13. Jesus had predicted both Jew and Gentile, indeed all the world, would hate and reject Him. Sin is evidence of that hatred. Still it stuns us to read of the brutality Jesus suffered at both trials, ecclesiastical and civil.

14. Pilate seems to understand the jealous motives of the Jews. John also clearly reveals their jealousy. They were envious of Jesus' miracles and the growing faith of His followers. They were jealous of their own position and power over the people (John 11:45–53).

15. Pilate's motives were no more pure than those of the others. Pilate's motives were also self-serving. He was in a precarious position politically. He faced permanent exile or forced suicide if he failed to handle successfully the volatile situation in Judea for Rome. He ignored the warnings of his own wife and allowed the crowd to manipulate him. He tried unsuccessfully to escape unscathed.

16. No one is innocent of Jesus' death. For every heart is turned in upon itself and away from God. We have only to look at our motives to see the sinful selfishness in our own heart. We build a kingdom there for ourselves. Jesus came to call us into His kingdom. He would be our sovereign Lord. It is through His death and resurrection that He sets us free from the tyranny of self. He draws us close to Himself, forgives and accepts us, and gifts us with faith to yield the throne of our heart to Him.

Day 5 • Matthew 27:32–66

17. **Challenge question.** Acts 6:9 indicates there were Jews in Cyrene. Perhaps Simon had come to Jerusalem to celebrate the Passover. This unexpected encounter with the execution party drew him into the center of the drama. Those condemned to death were usually forced to carry a beam of the cross, often weighing 30–40 pounds, to the place of crucifixion. Because Jesus was so weakened by flogging, He stumbled, and Simon was pressed into carrying the cross.

Perhaps Simon and his family became Christians. Mark refers to his sons, Rufus and Alexander, who must have been known later in Christian circles. And Paul refers to a Rufus and his mother and to their faith and love.

18. Jesus wanted to be fully conscious until His death. During the six hours of the crucifixion Jesus spent the first three hours praying for His enemies, responding to the dying thief, and comforting those He loved. He needed to be alert for this and to fulfill the Scriptures. Jesus showed He yielded His life deliberately; no one took it from Him against His will (John 10:17–18; Luke 23:46). Jesus, by an act of His will, died a victor, completing what He came to do. His loud cry left no doubt.

19. The Gospel writers do not dwell on Jesus' physical suffering. Yet other first-century authors vividly described the agony and disgrace of crucifixion. And archaeologists' discoveries have shed light on the unnatural position of a body impaled with heavy nails through wrists and heel bones. Jesus quotes the first verse of Psalm 22 in His agony from the cross. Matthew and John see the passion of Jesus as the fulfillment of the cry of the psalm's righteous sufferer, encircled by enemies, flesh torn, bones out of joint, circulation restricted until the heart faints, dehydrated by fever and thirst, pierced in hands and feet, naked, and humiliated.

20. The cry from Jesus is a cry of need, a prayer for help, yet it is a cry of faith, for Jesus calls the Father "My God" *(Eloi)*. (Those who heard Him confused the word with Elijah, celebrated in Judaic legend as a helper in time of need.) Jesus confidently yields His spirit into the Father's keeping until the resurrection (Luke 23:46).

21. Invite members of the group to share insights, reaffirmations, and questions.

Notes

The Resurrected Lord Sends Disciples with the Gospel

Matthew 28

Preparing for the Session

Central Focus

Everyone has a story to tell. The story of discipleship that we tell is a witness commissioned by our living and exalted Lord Jesus Christ.

Objectives

That the participant, as a child of God and with the Holy Spirit's help, will be led to

1. be reminded that not all know and trust Jesus as the Messiah;
2. sharpen his or her witness to the historical resurrection of Jesus;
3. contrast the lowly Christ of earthly ministry to the same Christ in His exalted state;
4. learn some of the unique qualities of discipleship;
5. go and make disciples.

For the Small-Group Leader

The agenda for discussion groups in this last meeting of the present course includes three sections. First, we study Matthew 28—Matthew's account of Jesus' resurrection and of the Great Commission. Second, we examine New Testament passages that help us think about the implications flowing for us from Jesus' resurrection. Third, we review what we have gained from our study of Matthew.

Allow sufficient time for the third part. Encourage group members to express the ways in which they have grown from their LifeLight study so far. Such an exchange provides a satisfying conclusion to an episode of personal growth. It affirms the experience in the student's own awareness. And it rubs off on others.

Encourage members of your group to enroll in the next LifeLight course. If possible, distribute enrollment information or applications. Keep the LifeLight spirit going and growing!

Small-Group Discussion Helps

Day 1 • Matthew 28:1–10

1. Mary Magdalene and "the other Mary" (mother of James and Joses and wife of Clopas) were the first to see the open tomb. Mary Magdalene is mentioned in Luke 8:2–3. Luke describes her as having been healed of seven evil spirits. These women were among the group of women who traveled with Jesus and the disciples and used their own resources to help them. They watched Jesus' burial, sitting opposite the tomb. At dawn the next morning, they found the tomb empty. Highlight the devotion of the women and the honor they were given as the first to announce Jesus' resurrection.

2. (a) The imperatives given by the angel: Fear not! Look! Believe! Go! Tell! Remember! (Today's English Version of the Bible). Jesus repeats: Fear not! Go! Tell! Jesus' greeting to the women on the road was *Chairete*, the normal word of greeting, whose literal meaning is "Rejoice!"

(b) These imperatives are wonderfully encouraging to the women and to us. Now that Jesus has risen from the dead and sin, death, and Satan have been conquered, there is nothing to fear. We have seen with our own eyes and minds and hearts in this study of Matthew's Gospel that Jesus is the true promised Messiah, God's Son and the ruler of the Kingdom. The resurrection is the final seal of His victory. No wonder, then, Jesus greets the women with the command to rejoice! Joy and faith replace fear and despair. The Good News cannot be contained. With the women we will rush with speedy feet to go and tell.

(c) It is significant that the angel urges the women (v. 6a) to remember Jesus' own prediction of His resurrection, to base their faith on His word to them. They have Jesus' own word. Although they see with their own eyes (v. 6b), they are urged not to hesitate but to take Jesus at His word.

3. Although they had forsaken and denied Him, Jesus calls the disciples His brothers (v. 10). He seems eager to see them and promises to meet them in Galilee.

4. (a) Ask for personal responses to this question. In His encounter with the women Jesus seems to convey His own joy. He wants them to share His joy. The battle is finished. The victory is won! He assures them; He removes their fear; He sends them on a mission.

(b) The women's response is a mixture of joy and fear. Seeing Jesus themselves and meeting Him on the road must have been thrilling beyond words. Perhaps they were speechless with joy and fear. Yet they didn't hesitate to come close to Him, touch Him, and worship Him.

(c) Help participants compare the women's response with their own during this study of Matthew.

Day 2 • Matthew 28:11–15

5. (a) Only Matthew tells of the posting of the guard and their report. (b) Although the guards at the tomb apparently witnessed what the women witnessed, it produced only fear, certainly no joy! They trembled with fear. Perhaps they fainted into unconsciousness. Fear, not faith, sent them to report to the chief priests and elders. (c) As for the chief priests, they were concerned only about covering up the resurrection of Jesus by falsifying what had happened. They persisted in their unbelief and in their hatred of Jesus despite the evidence of His resurrection.

6. The hearts of these chief priests and elders were so hardened that they refused to believe even in the face of the eyewitness account brought by the guards. Jesus indicated that even resurrection (was He hinting at just this response to His own resurrection?) would be met by stubborn denial by such a hardened heart. No wonder the writer of the epistle to the Hebrews warns us about such a hardening (Hebrews 3:7–15)!

7. It might seem that the plan of the chief priests worked, in that the majority of Jewish people did not then, and have not yet, come to believe that Jesus rose from the dead or is the Messiah. But ultimately no puny human attempt to discredit and sidetrack the Father's will can succeed. The Gospel is greater. The Father will have His way.

Day 3 • Matthew 28:16–20

8. (a) Jesus has proved His authority on earth by forgiving sins, healing broken bodies, completing the work of redemption by dying in the sinners' stead, and rising from death as conqueror. The Father gave Jesus the authority to do this and Jesus, as the Suffering Servant-King, obeyed and fulfilled the Father's will.

(b) Jesus expresses His compassion in His authoritative directives to the disciples. They are to go to all people everywhere. Jesus extends His mercy to all. Jesus gives the grace of Baptism and the gift of teaching. Jesus promises His presence.

9. Disciples are made by baptizing them and teaching them. The Word and Sacraments are the means the Holy Spirit uses to create faith (Ephesians 2:8–9). And it is the Holy Spirit who produces the fruits of faith (Ephesians 2:10; Galatians 5:22–23).

10. (a) "Baptized into [the name of the triune God]" implies that by Baptism we are received into communion with Him. In Baptism God is committed to us as our Father; the Son is our Savior; and the Spirit is the life-giving power in our lives (1 Corinthians 6:11; Galatians 3:26–27).

(b) We are committed to God in our Baptism through faith (Mark 16:16). Our faith, God's gift to us, commits us to Him—to listen to Him, trust Him, and follow Him.

11. (a) If we take our cue from these accounts of discipling found in Acts, we will know our job descriptions. We will share the Gospel by preaching the way of salvation, by responding to human need in Jesus' name (and then directing those we help to Jesus the Savior), and by using every opportunity (even adverse circumstances) to share Jesus with others, including one-on-one opportunities. We can't make someone else believe,

obey, or become committed to Jesus, but we can introduce others to the Savior we know, trust, and follow.

(b) Jesus directs us to go and share the Gospel, the only way to salvation and eternal life. The Gospel offers real life in a decaying and dying world. It's too good not to share.

(c) Jesus' enemy would rid the world (and us) of this precious Gospel. Having Jesus and His unconditional love close keeps us going—spreading and sharing, speaking and showing the Good News until Jesus returns.

Day 4 • Selected Verses from the Epistles

In this exercise you will want to guide your group to see how Jesus' resurrection affects our attitudes and actions in daily life.

12. That Christ now lives is proof that God accepted Jesus' death as full payment for sin and that He no longer regards us as enemies but as friends.

13. Just as Jesus' cross did away with our sins, so sin's power over us is now put behind us by Jesus' resurrection. By faith we died with Christ, and by faith we now live with Christ. Sin was defeated by Christ, and since by faith we died and rose with Him, sin no longer is our master. We do not have to be slaves of sin any longer.

14. The same Holy Spirit who raised Jesus from the dead also lives in us. That power is available to us—the same power that raised Jesus! That power enables us to believe and to live a godly life.

15. Because Jesus rose from death and lives forever in the glory of heaven, I also will rise from death and live forever with Him and all believers in glory. My own body will rise—in a changed, glorified state—to live again. This is my certainty, and the certainty of every believer, as I face death.

16. God can raise the dead! He has done it, and He will do it again! He raised Jesus from death, and He can and will raise me too, even if I should lose my life for His sake. How this truth must have encouraged countless martyrs! It can encourage us also, whether we face persecution or a life-threatening illness.

17. Most people don't like the thought of aging. We sometimes worry about the loss of physical and mental powers. What if I become a victim of multiple sclerosis or Alzheimer's disease? Even the prospect of a slow and certain degeneration of body and mind cannot extinguish the power of God, who "raised the Lord Jesus from the dead" and who "will also raise us with Jesus" (2 Corinthians 4:14).

18. The resurrected, living Christ now lives in me. "The life I live in the body, I live by faith in the Son of God, who loved me and gave Himself for me" (Galatians 2:20). I am now His hands and His feet, doing His will in this world. The life which I had selfishly claimed for myself is long gone. The only life I now have is Christ living in me.

19. I am living testimony to God's grace in Jesus. The fact that I live now by faith and will live in glory is all to the credit of Jesus. The good works I do are Jesus' doing, and the glory that I shall have in heaven will also be Jesus' doing. I am nothing on my own, but I am altogether a living exhibit of Jesus' grace and power.

20. Paul expresses the desire to experience personally the power of God that raised Jesus from death as he endures suffering as Jesus' servant. Experiencing that power, Paul also will triumph in suffering and be raised as Jesus was. We also desire this power, that we may triumph in our sufferings and have our share in the resurrection to eternal life in heaven.

21. Because we have been raised to a new life now with Jesus through faith, we desire to be with Him in heaven also. Paul expresses this desire for himself (Philippians 1:23). We also yearn for heaven and the indescribable joys that are waiting for us there.

Day 5 • Matthew 28:1–20

22. (a) You will want members to share individual responses. Have participants viewed Jesus in a new light? What have they learned about Jesus that they didn't know before? Have they noted Matthew's description of Jesus as promised Messiah, Son of David, Son of God, Suffering Servant, and New Israel? (b) Do members of your group recognize that the kingdom of God

is in every heart that believes? (c) Do they view Jesus' ministry on earth as a call to repentance, faith, and discipleship? Do they understand how Jesus fulfilled the promises of God and was obedient to the Father's will? Have they seen His compassion and mercy at work in the service of sinners?

23. Jesus calls us to share His ministry—to invite others to faith in Jesus, to exercise His compassion, to share the mercy we have received.

Ask group members to think of how they can serve others in these ways in the context of their daily lives—in specific places and with people closest to them. Ask them to think of ways to share Jesus' ministry along with their congregation and synod.

24. Every forgiven sinner, full of faith in Jesus by the power of His Spirit, evidences the truth that Jesus is truly alive!

25. One more time—invite group members to share insights and questions. Close with a prayer of thanksgiving for your growth together.

Notes